CW00499536

THE FISH AROUND MALTA

(Central Mediterranean)

GUIDO G. LANFRANCO

Progress Press Co. Ltd.
Malta
1996

Printed & Published by
Progress Press Co. Ltd.
1993

First Reprint 1996

ISBN 99909-3-003-1

CONTENTS

I dedicate this work
to my past biology students

PRELIMINARIES

Fish life

The present publication follows and replaces the three editions of my previous work ''A Complete Guide to the Fishes of Malta''. This was of course only complete so far as it listed the fish recorded in our waters till that time, but our list cannot remain stable for long, as new species can be encountered using present methods of underwater exploration, especially in deeper waters. In addition there are some fish reaching the central Mediterranean from the Red Sea, and others, once common have either disappeared or are becoming scarce. The modern problems of pollution are complex and have contributed greatly to the diminishing fish fauna, together with overfishing. Legislation, local and international, should impose restrictions on mesh size and type of nets used, quantities taken, closed seasons for certain species, prohibited areas and species taken, with an eye not only on the conservation of endangered species and allowing fish to reach breeding size, but also to ensure a supply for the future, whilst further efforts to consolidate and increase the lately introduced fish culture may be the best way out in the future.

Visits to our fish markets can be very fruitful in finding some unusual specimens especially in the assorted trays of non-migratory fish, as is also communicating with amateur and professional fishermen. I have found it of interest to examine the stomach contents of both sedentary and migrtory fish, as this often reveals elusive species and sheds light on their habits.

Basing interpretations on the study of the body of a dead fish can give some general information on its habits, even though it may not have been seen alive. A fish with a forked caudal fin with elongated lobes, is a fast swimmer. If fast, then it has a streamlined body and is usually migratory. If migratory it will form shoals, and these keep to the upper, open regions of the water; in fact, they are captured with surface nets. Inhabiting the upper waters, these fish are not colourful, but usually bluish black dorsally and silvery on the underside, thus harmonising with the water if seen from above or from beneath. Fish with a rounded or straight cut caudal fin are relatively slow, therefore not usually migratory, often sedentary, and thus they can be of various shapes and above all can afford to be colourful or dark amongst the rocks and seaweeds and the play of light in the lower regions of the sea. Fish with a body flattened dorso-ventrally are obviously bottom fish, and would not be streamlined for speed, so usually rest on the sea bottom. All the above would reveal, in their stomachs, species of fish, algae, and other organisms, depending on their diet, and level of activity.

Nomenclature

Although in my previous editions I had included various synonymous scientific names for general information, I now include such additional technical names only if they were used by previous writers on local fish fauna, for reference, and the initials of these authors are enclosed in brackets with each name. In most cases these are synonymous terms, but some are actually names of different, but similar or closely related species which had been erroneously identified, and now found to refer to some other species. English names have many synonyms, but only one principal name is given here, and very rarely a secondary name. The principal Maltese name is in italics. An examination of Maltese names will show that these fall into four categories, that is, fish having: (a) one, clear, traditional, standard name.

(b) a Maltese name identical to that of a separate, different species or more than one species. (c) more than one Maltese name for one species. (d) no known Maltese name. For the second category I have added a qualifying adjective to distinguish between the species, because it is untenable, illogical pointless and confusing to call known different species by the same name. For the third category I have adopted the name most insisted upon by previous authors and fishermen, or if it also falls under category two, have added a qualifying adjective to distinguish differences. For those in category four, where there is no known Maltese name, I have used one which, in my opinion, is most suited for reference purposes, because since a fish exists and is known, it should be called by some name. As with the scientific names, I have here also enclosed in brackets the initials of authors using the various Maltese name. Where no initials are given, it would mean that the name has been given or modified as justified in the above categories.

Text descriptions

I have dispensed with elaborate descriptions in the text, but have kept to obvious external features, supplemented by the illustrations, which I have entirely redrawn, basing them on various photographs, preserved specimens and personal notes and sketches. The illustrations are not drawn to scale. When consulting the diagrams note the position, relationships and proportions of fins and body, but remember that most fishes change certain features, as the head profile, with age. Details of fishing methods and utilisation have also been excluded, since these would require a volume on their own, and the aim of this work is mainly as a guide to fish identification and enumeration.

Main chararcters for each family are briefly given, including a general key to the species listed, and here, distinguishing characters have been restricted to visible external features only. Statements regarding frequency are only relative and general, since this is unstable, and depends on when, by whom, and by what methods sightings or captures are made, besides the possibility of occasional or periodic fluctuations in fish populations, due to natural changes in environmental conditions and food availability.

Abbreviations

Abbreviations in the text are the following: Fam. = family of fish. M. = Maltese name(s). E. = English name. Pl. = Plate number for illustration. + = more or bigger, refering to size above average. For brevity, when refering to fins in the text, their name is given as dorsal, caudal, anal, pectorals, pelvics, without using the word fin(s).

Reference initials

Of various published works and lists involving the fish around the Maltese Islands, those shown hereunder are being used as reference for the present work in relation to scientific names, Maltese names and records, using the initials indicated. These initials are not necessarily those of the proper name and surname of the author, but may also take other forms to suit our reference purposes. Other lists or works which do not offer any new aspect or material are not included. This list, therefore is not to be taken as a complete bibliography on local fish, but only as reference for the present work.

GT Trapani, Gaetano "A Catalogue of the Different Kinds of Fish of Malta and Gozo" Malta 1838.
GR Gulia, Gavino "Index Methodicus Melitensium

Piscum'' in ''Repertorio di Storia Naturale'' Malta 1858-1862.

GAVG Gulia, Gavino ''Tentamen Ichthyologie Melitensis...'' Malta 1861.

GB Gulia, Gavino ''Ittiologia Maltese; Scienidae'' in ''Il-Barth'' Malta 1871-1877.

GIOG Gulia, Giovanni ''Addition a La Faune Ichthyologique Maltaise'' in ''Bull.Soc.Zool.France'' Tom.XXXIV France 1909.

GD Despott, Giuseppe ''The Ichthyology of Malta'' Malta 1919. These initials also include, for our purposes, GDO, Omologazione delle voci dei mercati del pesce di Malta e Gozo'' Rome 1934, by the same author, which can be said to be an identical list except for a few ommissions.

RC Clark, Robert ''Rays and Skates, A Revision of the European Species'' H.M.S.O. London 1926.

GL Lanfranco, Guido ''A Complete Guide to the Fishes of Malta'' Malta 1958, 1965, 1974.

JB Barbara, Joe ''Ismijiet tal-Ħut tal-Mediterran'' Malta 1961.

BB Bertram, B.C.R. ''The Behaviour of Maltese fish by Day and Night'' in Underwater Assoc. of London Report 1965.

GJ Jennings, G.H. ''Mediterranean Fishes'' London 1979.

JC Cilia, Joseph L. ''Fishes at Il-Qawra tad-Dwejra, Gozo'' in ''Potamon'' No.3, Malta 1979.

VJ Jaccarini, Victor. Unpublished list submitted to Jos. Aquilina author of ''Maltese-English Dictionary'' Vol.1 1987, Vol.2 1990, Malta, as references and incorporated in that work.

JLC Cilia, Joseph L ''Some Previously Unrecorded Blennidae and Gobidae from Maltese Waters'' in ''The Central Mediterranean Naturalist'' Vol.2(1). Malta 1990.

A NOTE ABOUT THE AUTHOR

Guido Lanfranco was born at Sliema in 1930. He became a teacher in 1950 and after teaching in primary schools until 1964 he started to teach the sciences geography and advanced biology in various secondary and technical schools in Malta and Gozo, before settling to teach sixth form biology. For several years he also lectured at St. Michael's College of Education for Men Teachers on the methods of science teaching and social studies. In 1980 he was appointed assistant head and head of biology department in the New Lyceum, Msida, now renamed Upper Lyceum G.F.Abela, until his retirement in 1991.

He has written hundreds of articles and has broadcast numerous talks and television programmes on local natural history, history and horticulture, besides giving very frequent lectures on the same subjects to numerous interested bodies and societies.

He was active on the committees of many cultural societies in Malta, and became president of most of them, as The Geographical Society, The Cactus and Succulents Society, The Ornithological Society, The Science Teachers Association, Church models Association and others, and is still president of the Malta Folklore Society, besides having been president of the Natural History Soceity of Malta (now Society for the Study and Conservation of Nature) which he founded in 1962. For several years he was also on the council of the Malta Union of Teachers, on the committee of Din L-art Ħelwa (National Trust), The Malta Historical Soceity, etc... At one time he edited "The Teacher, the "Kakti u Sukkulenti Oħra" and still edits "L-Imnara". He has written several books, including several editions of "Guide to the Flora of Malta, "Field Guide to the Wild Flowers of Malta, and "Complete Guide to the Fishes of Malta", besides "Duwa u Semm fil-Ħxejjex Maltin" (on medicinal plants), and "Maltese Mammals". Others are ready or being prepared for publication.

He has organised many exhibitions for various societies, including Titular Statues, Lay Confraternities, History of Local Transport, Aspects of Maltese Folklore, Folk Medicine in Malta, others on local nature and folklore, and several on botanical art, for the first time in Malta. An exhibition of a hundred of his paintings of local wild flowers was also held in 1989. In 1969 he was awarded the bronze medal of merit by the Federation of Civic Committees for his work to the community.

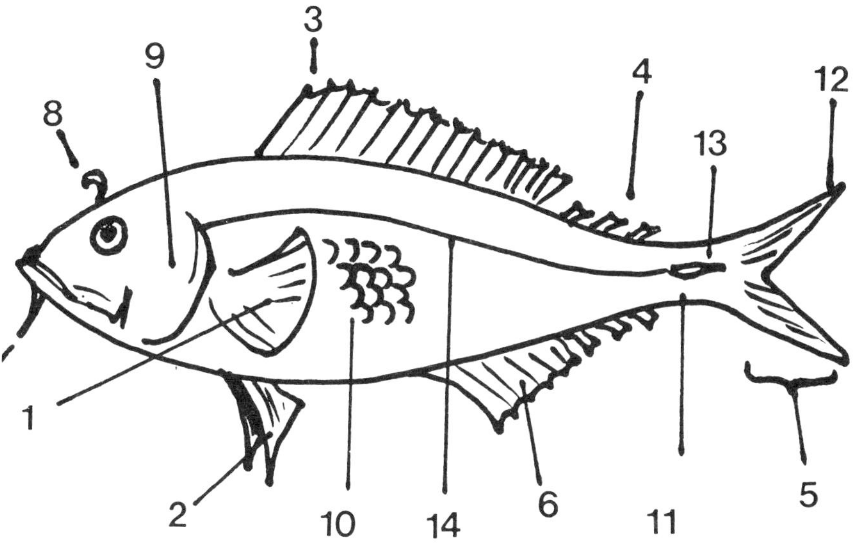

IDEALISED DIAGRAM TO SHOW PRINCIPAL, EXTERNAL FEATURES

1. PECTORAL FIN
2. PELVIC (or Ventral) FINS
3. DORSAL FIN
4. FINLETS
5. CAUDAL FIN
6. ANAL FIN
7. BARBEL
8. TENTACLE
9. OPERCULUM (Gill cover)
10. SCALES COVERING BODY
11. TAIL
12. TAIL LOBE
13. RIDGE OR KEEL ON TAIL SIDE
14. LATERAL LINE

THE FISH AROUND MALTA

(Central Mediterranean)

Phylum Chordata

Invertebrate chordate: 1; Vertebrate chordates: 2 to 288.

Chordates with cartilaginous endoskeleton and no operculum over gill openings: 2 to 53.

Chordates with bony endoskeleton and operculum covering gills: 54 to 288.

Fam Branchiostomidae

1. **Branchiostoma lanceolatum** (Pall). Branchiostoma lanceolatum (GIOG-1, GL-1); M. *Anfijossu*. E. Lancelet, Amphioxus.5-6cm. Body transparent, laterally compressed, greyish, on sandy bottoms, shallow water. Rare. Pl.1.

Fam. Petromyzonidae

2. **Petromyzon marinus** Linn. Petromyzon lampreda(GT) Petromyzon marinus (GAVG-1, GB, GD-1, GL-2); M. *Qalfat*. Qalfat (GT, GAVG-1, B, GD-1, GL-2); Buwaħħal (GT, GL-2); Sangisug?(GL-2). E. Sea Lamprey. 50-90cm.+. No jawbones; mouth a sucking disc; parasitic, attaching to fish, dolphins etc.sucking blood. Greeninsh, yellowish, greyish, mottled or marbled; pale underside. Dorsal edged black. Rare. Pl.1.

Fam. Hexanchidae

One spineless dorsal, 7 gill slits: 3; One spinelss dorsal, 6 gill slits: 4.

3. **Heptranchias perlo** (Bonn.). Heptanchus cinereus (GR, GAVG-170, GB, GD-3, GL-4) Heptranchus perlo(JB, VJ); M.*Murruna ta' seba*

garġi. Murruna(GR, GAVG-170, GB, GD-3, GL-4, JB). Morruna(GL-4). E. Seven-gilled shark. 80-135cm.+. Grey brownish often blotched darker; underside paler. Dorsal tipped black, caudal upper edge black. Not common. Pl.1.

4. **Hexanchus griseus** Bonn. Squalus griseus(GT), Hexanchus griseus (GR, GAVG-169, GB, GD-2, GL-3, JB, VJ) M. *Murruna b'sitt garġi*. Murruna (GT, GR, GAVG-169, GB, GD-2, GL-3, JB), Morruna (GL-3), Murruna b'sitt garġi (VJ). E. Blunt-nosed six-gilled shark. 2-4m.+. Dark grey or brown, lighter underside. Occasional, deep water. Pl.1.

Fam. Odontaspidae

No grooves between nares and mouth. 5 gillslits before origin of pectoral, 2 dorsals: 5; 5 gillslits before origin of pectorals, 2 dorsals, anal taller than 2nd dorsal: 6.

5. **Eugomphodus taurus** (Raf.). Odontaspis taurus (GB, GD-16, GL-11), Charcarias taurus (JB). M. *Tawru*. Kelb il-baħar (GL-11), Tawru (JB, GL-11). E. Sand tiger shark. 2-3m. Greyish brown, with or without yellowish or brownish irregular spots. Teeth usually 3-pointed. rare. Pl.1.

6. **Odontaspis ferox** (Riss). Odontaspis ferox (GR, GAVG-166, GB, GD-15, GL-10); Charcarias ferox (JB). M. *Silfjun*. Silfjun (GD-15, GL-10, JB); Kelb salvaġġ (GL-10). E. Small-tooth sand tiger. 3-3.5m. Brownish, greyish, with some irregular black spots; underside lighter. Pupil greenish. Caudal with dark edges. Teeth genrally 5-pointed. Occasionally close to shore. Rare. Pl.1.

Fam. Lamnidae

Second dorsal and anal very small; tail ridged at sides; 2 dorsals; 5 gill-slits before pectorals. Body stout, no teethlet at base of teeth: 7; body slender: 8; body stout, teeth with teethlets at base: 9.

7. **Carcharodon carcharias** (Linn.) Squalus carcharias (GT); Carcharodon carcharias (GD-19, GL-7, JB); Carcharinus lamia (GD-11, GL-16); Carcharodon lamia (GAVG-165, GB). M. *Kelb il-baħar abjad*. Kelb il-baħar (GT, GD-11, GL-16); Silfjun (GAVG-165); Ħuta tax-xmara (GB, GD-19, GL-7); Kelb il-baħar abjad (GL-7); Kelb abjad (JB). E. Great white shark. 5-7m.+. teeth finely serrated. Greyish, brownish, bluish, paler when young; pale below; black spot at base of pectorals. Dangerous to man; deep water, but occasionally inshore. Rare. Pl.1.

8. **Isurus oxyrinchus** Raf. Oxyrrhinus spallanzani (GR, GB);Lamna oxyrhynchus (GD-18); Isurus oxyrinchus (GL-6, JB, VJ). M. *Pixxitondu*. Pixxiplamtu (GR); Pixxitondu (GB); Pixxitondu (GD-18, GL-6, JB, VJ). E. Short-fin mako shark. 3-4m.+. Dark greyish blue or blue, underside white, eyes oval. At all depths; dangerous to man. Frequent. Pl.2.

9. **Lamna nasus** (Bonn.) Lamna cornubica (GAVG-167, GB, GD-17); Lamna nasus (JB, GL-5, VJ). M. *Pixxiplamtu*. Pixxiplamtu (GD-17, GL-5, JB, VJ). E. Porbeagle shark. 2-3m.+. Greyish or dark blue, whitish below, fins pale at base, eyes rounded. Deep water, sometimes associated with tunny and mackerel shoals. Rare. Pl.2.

Fam. Cetorhinidae

Five extremely long gill-slits, 2 dorsals, ridge on side of tail, teeth relatively tiny and numerous.

10. **Cetorhinus maximus** (Gunn.) Squalus lamia (GT); Squalus maximus (GT); Cetorhinus maximus (GD-20, GL-8, JB). M. *Gabdoll*. Pixxitonnu (GT, GD-20); Gabdoll (GT, GL-8, JB). E. Basking shark. 5-10m.+. Greyish, brownish, dark; pale blotches on side and lighter underside. Feeds only on small organisms. Teeth not serrated. Rare. Pl.2.

Fam. Alopiidae

Upper tail lobe as long as body; 5 gill-slits, 2 dorsals.

11. **Alopias vulpinus** (Bonn.). Alopecias vulpes (GR, GAVG-168); Alopias vulpes (GB, GD-14, GL-9); Alopias vulpinus (JB). M. *Pixxivolpi*. Budenb (GL-9); Pixxivolpi (GD-14, GL-9, JB). E. Thresher shark. 4-5m. Dark blackish-blue, greyish, brownish. Abdomen white, often mottled. Feeds on small organisms. Teeth unequal, not serrated. Sometimes frequent. Pl.2.

Fam. Scyliorhinidae

No keel on side of tail; 2 spineless dorsals; 5 gill slits, the last 2 overlapping origin of pectorals: 12, 13, 14; distinguished by means of colour pattern.

12. **Galeus melanostomus** Raf. Scyllium melanostomum (GAVG-162, GB); Pristiurus melanostomus (GR, GD-6, GL-14); Galeus melanostomus (JB). M. *Gattarell ħalqu iswed*. Gattarell (GAVG-162); Gattarell ħalqu iswed (GR, GB, GD-6, GL-14); Ċamperlina (JB,

GL-14). E. Blackmouth cat-shark. 50-90cm. Mouth interior black; back and sides greyish, dark blotches isolated by pale lines; whitish below; eyes green. Frequent. Pl.2

13. **Scyliorhinus canicula** (Linn). Squalus catulus (GT); Scyllium canicula (GAVG-160, GR, GB); Scylliorhinus canicula (GD-5, GL-13, JB). M. *Gattarell tat-tikek.* Gattarell (GT, GR, GAVG-160, GB, GD-5, GL-13, JB). E. Small-spotted cat shark. 0.60-1.00m. Ochre grey, spıotted with small, dark blotches and spots; underside white; muddy bottoms, often close inshore. Frequent. Pl.3.

14. **Scyliorhinus stellaris** Linn. Squalus stellaris (GT); Squalus stellare (GR, GAVG-161, GB); Scyllium catulus (GR); Schliorhinus stellaris (GD-4, JB, GL-12). M. *Gattarell tar-rukkal.* Qattus tar-rukkal (GT); Gattarell tar-rukkal (GAVG-161, GB, GD-4, GL-12, JB); Gattarell tal-blat (GL-12). E. Nursehound. 1.0-1.70m. Colour variable, usually pale with body covered with medium-sized, dark blotches and spots interspersed with still smaller dots, less densely packed than in the preceding species. Frequent rocky bottoms, clear water. Pl.3.

Fam. Carcharhinidae

Five gill slits, the 3rd being longest and 5th shortest and overlaps the origin of the pectoral; 2 dorsals. Body robust, elevated, pectoral length X2 of 1st dorsal: 15; body slender, pectoral length X3 of 1st dorsal: 16.

15. **Carcharhinus plumbeus** (Nardo) Carcharhinus plumbeus (JB). M. *Kelb griż.* Kelb griż (JB). E. Sandbar shark (/Large-finned shark). 2-3m. Upper teeth serrated and white, lower teeth very narrow with a wide base. Body grey, greenish brown, underside whitish. Often frequent.

NOTE: Carcharhinus brevipinnis (Mull & Henl.), E. Spinner shark, 1.50-2.70m, with 1st dorsal shallow in relation to body height, and well behind pectoral, and body greyish-brownish without markings, may be met with. Occasional reports of sharks leaping out of water should refer to this species or **C. limbatus** (Val.), E. Blacktip spinner shark, also unmarked body, but with black fin tips, except the anal, 1.50-2.50m, appearing similar to C. melanopterus (Q, & G.) E. Black tip reef shark, 1.0-1.75m, which has 1st dorsal, anal and lower caudal tipped black. These last three sharks are occasionally sighted, but are rather confusing to identify, having overlapping characteristrics.

16. **Prionace glauca** (Linn.) Galeus glaucus (GR, GAVG-164); Squalus glaucus(GB); Prionace glauca (GD-10, GL-15, JB). M. *Ħuta kaħla.* Kelb il-baħar (GR, GAVG-164, GB); Ħuta kaħla (GD-1), GL-15, JB).

E. Blue shark. 2.50-3.0m. +. Dark blue, white below; 4 rows of teeth in upper jaw, smooth in small specimens, serrated in larger. Frequent. Pl.3.

Fam. Triakidae

Five, short, equal gill slits, the last two overlapping origin of pectorals; 2 dorsals. Teeth of both jaws similar: 17; teeth not similar in both jaws, body spotted white: 18; teeth not the same in both jaws, body not spotted white: 19.

17. **Galeorhinus galeus** (Linn.) Galeus galeus (GD-10, GL-17, JB). M. *Kelb il-baħar*. Mazzola (GD-10, GL-17); Mazzola bla xewka (GL-17);Kelb il-baħar (GL-17, JB). E. Tope shark. 1.50-2.0m. +. Dark greyish-bluish, paler in larger specimens. Teeth equal, small, serrated. Frequent. Pl.3.

18. **Mustelus asterias** Coq. Squalus galeus (GT); Galeus canis (GAVG-163, GB); Mustelus canis (GR, GD-7, GL-19); Mustelus asterias (JB, VJ). M. *Mazzola tat-tbajja*. Mazzola bla xewka (GT, GAVG-163, GB, GD-7, GL-19); Mazzola (GL-19); Mazzola tat-tbajja (JB, VJ). E. Starry smooth hound. 0.80-1.30m. +. Variable, greenish-brownish with many white spots which are often faint; underside white. Common. Pl.3.

19. **Mustelus mustelus** (Linn.). Mustelus mustelus (GD-8, GL-18, JB). M. *Mazzola bla xewka*. Żagħrun (GD-8); Mazzola tat-tbajja (GL-18); Mazzola bla xewka (GL-18, JB). E. Smooth hound. 1.0-1.50m. Greyish-bluish, with slight black spots or streaks; very variable. Snout shorter than in foregoing species. Frequent. Pl.3.

Fam. Sphyrnidae

Head flattened and extended sideways into lateral projections, carrying the eyes to the tips. 5 gill slits, 2 dorsals. Pelvics start just after limits of 1st dorsal, nares not very close to eyes, body robust: 20; pelvics start far behind limits of 1st dorsal, nares close to eyes, body slender: 21.

20. **Sphyrna tudes** (Val.) Platysgnolus tuburo, Gulia (GB); Sphyrna tudes (GD-13, GL-21). M. *Kurazza rasha żgħira*. Krozza (GD-13); Kurazza, Pixximartell (GL-21). E. Small-eye hammerhead (/Lesser hammerhead). 1.0-1.50m. Head twice as wide as long; greyish-brownish; underside whitish. Sometimes considered to be juvenile of S.zygaena. Very rare. Pl.4.

21. **Sphyrna zygaena** (Linn.) Squalus zygaena (GT); Zygaena malleus (GR, GAVG-177, GB); Sphyrna zygaena (GD-12, GL-20). M. *Kurazza*

komuni. Kurazza (GT, GR, GAVG-177, GB, GD-12, GL-20); Pixximartell (GL-20). E. Smooth hammerhead shark. 3-4m. Head three times as wide as long; dark greenish, brownish greyish; underside white. Occasionally met with. Pl/4

Fam. Oxynotidae

Body humped, underside flat, narrow back, 5 very small gill slits; a strong, large spine runs vertically through the dorsal fins; abdomen with a skinny keel.

22. **Oxynotus centrina** Linn. Centrina salviani (GR, GAVG-173, GB, GD-25, GL-23); Oxynotus centrina (JB). M. *Pixxiporku*. Ġurdien il-baħar (GR, GAVG-173); Far (GB); Ġurdien (GB, GD-25, GL-23); Pixxiporku (JB, GL-23). E. Angular rough shark. 0.5-1.5m. Dark reddish brown, abdomen lighter; skin very rough; iris greenish. Frequent, deeper waters. Pl.4.

Fam. Squalidae

Nostrils not joined to mouth; 5 gill slits before origin of pectorals; 2 dorsals. Dorsals spiny, not close together, basal points very extended: 23; dorsals with small spine, not close together: 24; dorsals spineless, not close together, thick folds of skin around head and neck: 25; dorsals spineless, close to each other and close to caudal, 1st gill slit shortest, 5th longest: 26; dorsals spiny, not close together, gill slits small and equal: 27; dorsals spiny, not close together, body spotted white: 28; dorsals spiny, not close together, not spotted white: 29.

23. **Centrophorus granulosus** (Schn.) Centrophorus granulosus (GD-24, GL-27, JB, VJ). M. *Żagħrun*. Pixxinotte, Sagru (GL-27); Żagħrun (JB, GL-27, VJ). E. Gulper shark. 1.0-1.50m. Skin very rough, greyish or purplish brown, underside paler; fins with uneven edges; eyes comparatively large. Frequent. Pl.4.
24. **Centrophorus uyato** (Raf.) Spinax uyatus (GR, GAVG-172); Acanthus uyatus (GB). M. *Mazzola bix-xewka*. Mazzola bix-xewka (GB). E. Little gulper shark. 40-90cm.+. Dark brownish grey, fins dark with pale tips; underside whitish. Occasional. Pl.4.
25. **Dalatias licha** (Bonn.) Dalatias licha (JB). M. *Murruna sewda*. Murruna sewda (JB). E. Kitefin shark. 1.25-1.50m. All brown or grey with paler fin edges; 5th gill slit longest, 1st shortest; mouth region flabby. Frequent.

26. **Echinorhinus brucus** (Benn.) Echinorhinus spinosus (GAVG-174, GB, GD-26, GL-22). M. *Murruna tax-xewk*. Murruna xewwekija, Murruna tal-fosos (GL-22). E. Bramble shark. 2.0-2.25m+. Greyish purplish-brown with irregular spots, underside yellowish and paler; body robust, covered sparsely with protruding spiny tubercles. Not frequent. Pl.4.

27. **Etmopterus spinax** (Linn.) Etmopterus spinax (GD-23, GL-24, JB). M. *Mazzola tal-fanal*. Mazzola tax-xewka (GD-23, GL-24); Djavlu, Sagru, Mazzola tal-fond (GL-24). E. Velvet belly shark. 30-60cm+. Dark brown back, black underside, dark lateral line, flanks darkly blotched, often phosphorescent; interior of mouth black. Frequent occasionally, but rare most years. Pl.5.

28. **Squalus acanthias** (Linn.) Squalus acanthias (GT, GD-27, GL-25, JB); Spinax acanthias (GR, GAVG-71, GB). M. *Mazzola griża*. Mazzola bix-xewka (GT, GR, GAVG-171); Mazzola (GD-27, GL-25, JB). E. Spur dogfish. 60-100cm.+. Grey, with or without creamy spots. Frequent, often close inshore. Pl.5.

29. **Squalus blainvillei** (Riss.) Acanthias blainvillei (GB); Squalus blainvillei (GD-22); Squalus fernandinus (JB, GL-26). M. *Mazzola tax-xewka*. Ujatu (GL-26). E. Longnose spurdog. 60-100cm+. Greyish, brownish, underside white, fins margined white. Frequent. Pl.5.

Fam. Squatinidae

Body clongated and greatly flattened doso-ventrally, pectorals close to wide head extending sideways:

30. **Squatina oculata** Bon. Squatina ocellata (GR, GAVG-176); Squatina oculata (GB). M. *Xkatlu ta' l-Għajnejn*. Xkatlu (GR, GB). E. Smoothback angelshark. 1.0-1.5m. Greyish or reddish brown marked brownish and some regular white spots and some others large, dark, arranged longitudinally. Not frequent. Pl.5.

31. **Squatina squatina** (Linn.) Squatina angelus (GR, GAVG-175, GB); Squatina squatina (GD-27, GL-28, JB). M. *Xkatlu komuni*. Xkatlu (GR, GB, GD-27, GL-28, JB); Skwadru (GL-28). E. Angel shark. 0.50-2.00m.+. Olive brown-greyish brown with black spots and sparse, sharp denticles. Variable. Underside white. Frequent. Pl.5.

Fam. Pristidae

Snout extending into a bilateral saw; body dorso-ventrally compressed

32. **Pristis pristis** (Linn.) Pristis antiquorum (GR, GAVG-178, GB, GD-28,

GL-29); Squalus pristis (GT). M. *Sija*. Sija (GT, GR, GAVG-178, GD-28, GL-29); Pixxiserrieq, Pixxisega (GL-29). E. Sawfish. 3-4m.+. Yellowish grey, paler underside, and the characteristic double-sided saw extention of the upper jaw. Appears to be accidental and extremely rare in the Mediterranean.

Fam. Rhinobatidae

Flat, elongated body, anteriorly pointed. Wide groove from eyes to tip of snout: 33; narrow groove from eye to tip of snout: 34.

33. **Rhinobatos rhinobatos** (Linn.) Rhinobatus columnae (GB); Rhinobatus panduratus (GD-29, GL-33); Rhinobatos rhinbobatos (JB, VJ). M. *Vjolin*. Rebekkin (GB);Vjolin (GB, GD-29, GL-33, JB, VJ); Kuntrabaxx (GL-33). E. Common Guitarfish. 0.50-1.00m. Brownish-olive brown, or ochre-yellowish grey; pale below. Rare. Pl.5.
34. **Rhinobatos cemiculus** E.Geof. Rhinobatus halavi (GD-30, GL-34). R.halavi (GD-30, GL-34), appears to have been a misinterpretation of R.cemiculus. M. *Kuntrabaxx*. Kuntrabaxx (GD-30, GL-34). E. Blackchin guitarfish. 0.60-1.60m+. Brownish ochre with darker snout, which is larger than in R. rhinobatos. Not frequent.

Fam. Torpedinidae

Body flat, rounded, soft, capable of producing an electric shock. Space between dorsals shorter than their base, 1st dorsal taller than 2nd.: 35; space between dorsals shorter than their bases, 2nd dorsal nearly equal to 1st.: 36; space between dorsals equal or longer than their base, 2nd dorsal nearly equal to 1st.: 37.

35. **Torpedo(Tetronarce)nobiliana** Bon. Torpedo nobiliana (GD-40, GL-32, JB). M. *Haddiela sewda*. Haddiela samra, Haddiela mdahhna (GL-32); Haddiela sewda (JB, GL-32). E. Electric ray (/Dark torpedo). 0.50-1.50m.+. Dark purple brown, with or without tiny black or white dots; underside pale. Usually rare, occasionally frequent. Pl.6.
36. **Torpedo (Torpedo) marmorata** Riss. Raja torpedo (GT); Torpedo galvani (GR, GAVG-180, GB); Torpedo marmorata (GD-39, GL-30). M. *Ħaddiela komuni*. Ħaddiela (GT, GR, GAVG-180, GB, GD-39, GL-30); Ħaddiela tax-xokk (GL-30). E. Marbled electric ray. 40-60cm.+. Mainly brownish, very variable; hazy indistinct blotches; underside pale. Gives a more violent shock than its congeners. Frequent. Pl.6.

37. **Torpedo(Torpedo)torpedo** (Linn.) Torpedo narce (GR, GAVG-179, GB);Torpedo ocellata (GD-38, GL-31); Torpedo torpedo (JB). M. *Ħaddiela ta' l-għajnejn*. Ħaddiela (GR, GAVG-179); Ħaddiela mtebba' (GB); Ħaddiela ta' l-għajnejn (GB, GD-38, GL-31, JB). E. Common torpedo. 25-35cm+. Brownish ochre, variable, with occasionally 5 blue spots ringed black with a pale halo; underside pale. Often common. Pl.6.

Fam. Rajidae

Body very flat dorso-ventrally, forming a more or less lozenge-shaped disc; the pectorals extend sideways close to the head. Snout long, acutely pointed, ratio of space between eyes to length anterior to eyes 1:2 ; 38; snout very long, acutely pointed, ratio of space between eyes to length anterior to eyes 2:5 : 39; snout wide, pointed, ratio of space between eyes to length anterior to eyes 2:3 : 4O; snout tip elongated, ratio of space between eyes to length anterior to eyes 1:3 : 41; snout sahort and wide, ratio of space between eyes to space anterior to eyes 4:9 :42; snout wide and short, ratio of space between eyes to space anterior to eyes 1:2 :43; snout wide and short, ratio of space between eyes to space anterior to eyes 4:11 : 44; snout wide and short, head sides roundes, ratio of space between eyes to space anterior to eyes 1:2 : 45. Disc shape may vary with age. (sizes below, given for disc width).

38. **Raja (Dipturus) batis** Linn. Raja batis (GT, GR, GAVG-138, GD-34, GL-40, JB); Raja macrorhyncus (GD-33, GL-42). M. *Rebekkin skur*. Raja tar-ramel (GT, GR, GAVG-183, GD-34, GL-40); Rebekkin geddumu qasir (GD-33, GL-42); Rebekkin (GL-42); Rebekkin skur (JB, GL-40). E. Skate (/Smooth skate). 1-2m.+. variable olive-brown grey, with pale markings, dark blotches and hazy eye spot. Underside greyish. Not common. Pl.6.

39. **Raja(Dipturus)oxyrinchus** Linn. Raja oxyrinchus (GT, GD-32, RC, GL-41); Laeviraja oxyrhynchus (GR, GAVG-184, GB); Raja(Dipturus)oxyrinchus (VJ). M. *Rebekkin geddumu twil*. Rebekkin (GT, GR, GAVG-184, GL-41); Vjolin (GT, GR, GAVG-184, GD-32); Ħamiema (GB, GD-32, GL-41, VJ); Rebekkin ta' mnieħru twil (VJ). E. Longnose skate (/Sharpnosed skate). 0.50-1.00m.+. Variable, brownish greyish with light or dark spots or dots; underside dark, greyish, brownish, often paler. Frequent. Pl.6.

40. **Raja(Leucoraja)fullonica** Linn. Raja leucoraja fullonica (JB, VJ). M. *Raja petruża*. Raja petruża (JB, VJ). E. Shagreen ray. 0.50-1.00m. Characterised by uniform grey back; underside whitish. Apparently rare.

41. **Raja(Leucoraja)melitensis** Clark. Raja melitensis (RC, GDO, GL-39, VJ). M. *Raja ta' Malta*. Raja maltija (GDO); Raja ta, Malta (VJ). E. Maltese Brown ray. 40-50cm.+. Yellowish, brownish ochre; main spots on each side made up of yellowish ochre markings. There is a triangular patch of spines on back; whitish below. Very similar to R.naevus, Mull & Henl., which, however, is not yet recorded from Malta although in area. It can also be confused with forms of R.miraletus L. Frequent. Pl.6.

NOTE: Raja (Raja) brachyura Laf., listed by VJ, E. Blonde Ray, M. Raja batra (VJ), is a doubtful Mediterranean species.

42. **Raja(Raja)asterias** Del. Dasybatis asterias (GB); Raja punctata (GD-37, GL-37); Raja asterias (JB). M. *Raja tal-kwiekeb*. Raja (GB, GD-37); Raja tat-tikek, Raja ta' l-għajn (GL-37); Raja tal-kwiekeb (JB, GL-37). E. Starry ray. 50-60cm.+. Very variable, pale olive brown or yellowish green, with varying dark circles of spots around other whitish patches of spots. Underside white. Common. Pl.6.

43. **Raja(Raja)clavata** Linn. Raja clavata (GT, GR, GAVG-181, GD-31, RC, GL-35, JB); M. *Raja tal-fosos*. Raja petruża (GT, GR, GAVG-181); Raja tal-fosos (GB, GD-31, GL-35, JB). E. Thornback ray. 50-80cm.+. Back covered with spiny tubercles as also the underside of some adults; very variable, greyish, brownish spots, light and dark areas, with spaces forming paler or darker spots; underside lighter. Frequent. Pl.7.

44. **Raja (Raja) miraletus** Linn. Raja miraletus (GT, GR, GAVG-182, GB, GD-36, RC, GL-38, JB). M. *Raja lixxa*. Raja petruża (GR); Raja lixxa (GT, GAVG-182, GB, GD-36, GL-38, JB). E. Brown ray. 45-60cm.+. Yellow ochre brownish, with one characteristic, round or oval blue or purplish eyespot on each side circled yellowish and numerous dark spots. Whitish below. Frequent. Pl.7.

NOTE: **Raja (Raja) montagui** Fow., listed as R. maculata Montag. (GB) M. Raja petruża tar-ramel (GB), E. Spotted Ray, is of doubtful occurance, and may be referable to R. radula Del.

45. **Raja (Raja) radula** Del. Raja radula (GD-35, RC, GL-36, JB). M. *Raja tar-ramel*. Raja petruża (GL-36); Raja tar-ramel (GD-35, GL-36, JB). E. Rough ray. 50-60cm.+. Light-yellowish grey, marbled with greyish streaks and spots, with an eyespot on each side encircled yellow, often with a lighter centre; underside whitish. Frequent. Pl.7.

NOTE: **Raja (Rostroraja) alba** Lac. E. White skate, listed as M. *Ħamiema*. (JB, VJ) is a new record with distribution west/north Mediterranean.

Fam. Dasyatidae

Very flat body with extended pectorals; anterior body outline very obtuse; head level with body disc; tail with a dorsal spine; pectorals very wide and rounded. Back pigmented, underside white: 46; back pigmented, underside white framed dark: 47; back and underside both pigmented: 48. (measurements given below across disc.)

46. **Dasyatis centroura** (Mitch.) Dasyatis brucco (GD-42, GL-44); Dasybatis thalassia (GD-44, GL-46). M. *Boll denbu aħrax*. E. Rough tailed stingray. 0.80-1.00m+. Variable, brownish ochre with thorns along side and back of tail; underside pale. Rare. Pl.7.
47. **Dasyatis pastinaca** (Linn.) Raja pastinaca (GT); Trygon pastinaca (GR, GAVG-185, GB);Dasyatis pastinaca (GD-41, GL-43, JB). M. *Boll komuni*. Boll (GT, GR, GAVG-185, GB, GD-41, GL-43, JB); Sorċ (young) (GR, GAVG-185, GB); Ħamiema, Bonn, Ħamiema tas-sikkina (GL-43). E. Common stingray. 40-50cm.+. Variable, blackish, brownish ochre, often marbled; underside white with darker edges. Common. Pl.7.
48. **Dasyatis violacea** (Bon.) Trygon violacea (GB); Dasyatis violacea (GD-43, GL-45). M. *Boll vjola*. Boll tork (JB, GL-45);Boll vjola (GL-45). E. Violet stingray. 60-80cm.+. Uniform purplish, bluish, greenish blue; underside the same, but may be lighter. Mostly rare. Pl.7.

NOTE: Gymnura altavela Linn, E. Spiny butterfly ray, 1.50-3.0m.+, listed by JB M. *Farfett*.(JB), with disc twice as wide as long and relatively short tail, is sometimes reported.

Fam. Myliobatidae

Body flat, but above level of pectorals, which are very widely extended, pointed at the tips; head prominent, above and ahead of anterior disc outline and head with convex anterior outline. Dorsal originates after pelvic fins limits: 49; Dorsal in line with pelvics: 50.

49. **Myliobatis aquila** (Linn.) Raja aquila (GT); Myiliobatis aquila (GR, GAVG-186, GB, GD-45, GL-47, JB). M. *Ħamiema komuni*. Ħamiema (GT, GR, GAVG-186, GD-45, GL-47); Tajra, Għasfur (GL-47); Ajkla (JB, GL-47). E. Common eagle ray. 50-70cm.+. Variable, but usually brownish with greenish yellow; underside white. Frequent. Pl.7.
50. **Pteromylaeus bovinus** (Geoff.S.H.) Myliobatis bovinus (GD-46, GL-48, JB). M. *Ħamiema rasha twila*. Ħamiema (GD-46, GL-48); Għasfur (JB, GL-48); Tajra (GL-48). E. Bull ray. 0.80-1.30m+. Greenish, brownish or grey with darker, transverse bands, especially

visible in the smaller specimens; sometimes considered as a young form of M.aquila (L.). Frequent. PL.7.

Fam. Rhinopteridae

Similar to Myliobatidae, but anterior outline of head, seen dorsally, is concave; dorsal fin in line with pelvics.

51. **Rhinoptera marginata** (Geoff.S.H.) M. *Ħamiema kbira*. E. Lusitanian cownose ray. 1.50-2.0m. Brownish olive brown above, pale below. Occasionally reported. Usually mistaken for, and assumed to be Myliobatis aquila (L.) or Pteromylaeus bovinus (Geoff.S.H.).

Fam. Mobulidae

Body flat with laterally extended pectorals pointing backwards; 2 hornlike flaps extend forward on head sides, beyond eyes.

52. **Mobula mobular** (Bonn.) Cephaloptera giorna (GIOG-9); Cephaloptera adentula (GD-47); Mobula mobular (JB, GL-49). M. *Baqra*. Manta, Raja tal-qrun (GL-49); Baqra (GD-47, GL-49). E. Devil ray. 4-5m.+. Blackish brown or deep blue with greenish reflections, whitish below. Feeds on micro-organisms, harmless to man. Very rare. Pl.8

Fam. Chimaeridae

One gill opening; body tapering into whip-like tail, 1st dorsal with long, anterior spine. Body anteriorly bulky, dorsals and pectorals relatively large.

53. **Chimaera monstrosa** Linn. Chimaera monstrosa (GIOG-8, GD-48, GL-50, JB). M. *Fenek tal-baħar*. Ġurdien tal-baħar, Far tal-baħar (GD-48, GL-50); Fenek tal-baħar (GD-48, GL-50, JB). E. Rabbitfish. 50-70cm.+. Variable, with yellowish brown, silvery, and dark streaks and blotches; eyes greenish; males with an appendage on snout. Rare. Pl.8.

Family Acipenseridae

Body with rows of hard, bony projections; jaws toothless, one dorsal, 2 barbels under jaw.

54. **Acipenser sturio** Linn. Acipenser sturio (GT, GD-49, GL-51, JB). M. *Sturjun*. Sturjun (GT, GL-51, JB). E. Sturgeon. 1-2m.+. Variable, dull brown, greyish-yellowish. Very rare.

Fam. Clupeidae

One short dorsal; a row of coarse projections along abdomen; no lateral line. Slight bent groove on top of upper snout: 55; large scales, pelvics below middle of dorsal: 56; pelvics below hind half of dorsal: 57; pelvics below hind half of dorsal, and black spot on edge of operculum: 58; pelvics below origin of dorsal, no spot on operculum edge: 59.

55. **Alosa fallax** (Lac.) Clupea alosa (GT, GD-101); Alosa communis GR, GAVG-11); Alosa fallax nilotica (GL-54). M. *Laċċi tat-tbajja*. Laċċi (GT, GR, GAVG-11, GD-101, GL-54) Alosa, Laċċi tat-tbajja (GL-54). E. Twaite shad (/Allis shad). 25-50cm.+. Blue-green or blue with silvery sides and abdomen, with 6-7 dark spots on each side; ssp nilotica in Mediterranean often tinged metallic. Dorsal, caudal dark; pectorals, ventral and anal white. Frequent. Pl.8.

NOTE: **Alosa alosa** Linn. E. Allis shad, listed by JB as M. Laċċa, is a western Mediterranean species, and may have been refering to Alosa fallax.Lac. **Clupea harengus** Linn., E. Herring, listed by GT as M. Aringa, is not a Mediterranean species, but imported for retail.

56. **Sardina pilchardus** (Walb.) Clupea pilchardus (GT, GD-102); Clupea argyrochlora (GR, GAVG-8); Clupea sardina, Clupenodon sardina (GR, GAVG-10); Clupea chrysotaenia (GAVG-9); Clupea auro-vittata (GR); Sardina pilchardus (JB); Clupea pilchardus sardina (GL-53). M. *Sardina*.(adult), *Nemusa*. (young). Sardina, Nemusa (GR, GAVG-8, 9, GL-53); Saraga (GT, GD-102); Sarda (GL-53);Sardina kaħla JB, GL-53). E. European pilchard. Metallic or greenish blue, sides and underside silvery white, sometimes with dark markings along upper sides; operculae with golden reflections. Common in shoals, in bays and harbours. Pl.8.

57. **Sardinella aurita** Val. Engraulis desmaresti (GAVG-13); Clupea aurita (GD-103); Sardinella aurita (JB, GL-56). M. *Laċċa tal-faxx*. Nemusa (GAVG-13, GL-56); Sardina (GD-103, GL-56); Sarda, Laċċi, Laċċuna (GL-56); Laċċa tal-faxx (JB, GL-56). E. Round sardinella. 25-30cm. Dark blue or greenish, sides and underside silvery white with a blackish spot behind and above the operculum; A longitudinal, golden stripe often along each side. Dorsal brown, caudal grey striped black, other fins white. Not frequent. Pl.8.

58. **Sardinella maderensis** (Lowe.) Sardinella maderensis (VJ). M. *Laċċi tal-gewnaħ iswed*. Laċċi afrikana (VJ). E. Madeiran sardinella (Short-bodied sardine). 25-30cm. Robust body, blackish spot at base of dorsal and and black edge along pectorals. Frequent in migratory shoals. Apparently confused with its congeners and overlooked. Pl.8.

59. **Sprattus sprattus** (Linn.) Clupea sprattus (GT, GD-104, GL-55, JB); Clupea phalerica (GR); Clupenodon phalerica (GAVG-12); Sprattus sprattus sprattus (VJ). M. *Laċċi kaħla*. Sardina (GT, GD-104); Laċċi (GR, GD-104, GL-55); Sardinella, Sardina friska, (GL-55); Sardina ħadra (JB, GL-55); Sarda kaħla (VJ). E. Sprat. 7-14cm. +. Dark blue with green reflections; sides and underside silvery white, with or without bright bands. Irregular, but occasionally frequent. Pl.8.

Fam. Engraulidae

Snout projects forward above lower jaw; eyes large, close to snout; 1 dorsal, pelvic origin before that of dorsal;.

60. **Engraulis encrasicolus** (Linn.) Clupea encrasicolus (GT); Engraulis amara (GR,GAVG-15); Engraulis encrasicolus (GR,GAVG-13, GD-105,GL-57,JB). M. *Inċova*.(adult), *Nemusa*. (young). Inċova (GT,GR,GAVG-13,GD-105,GL-57); Nemusa (GT,GAVG-15, GD-105,GL-57,JB); Nemusa rasha morra (GR)). E. European anchovy. 10-20cm. Variable. Silvery dark bluish or dark green, usually with a bright, longitudinal silvery stripe on each side; underside lighter. Frequent. Pl.8.

Fam. Salmonidae

Salmo salar Linn, E. Atlantic salmon, listed by GT as M. Salamun, and as very rare, together with Salmo trutta Linn.,E. Brown trout, listed by GR,GAVG, as Salmo fario M. Salamun, also as very rare, should not form part of our fish fauna, as they are not in our area.

Fam. Argentinidae

Mouth small, not reaching eye outline; 2nd dorsal rudimentary.

61. **Argentina sphyraena** Linn. Argentina sphyraena (GD-117,GL-59,JB). M. *Arġentina*. Kurunetta (GL-59); Kurunella (JB,GL-59). E. Argentine. 15-25cm. +. Greenish, bluish, but silvery all over, abdomen lighter. A bright silvery band along each side; scales relatively large. Caudal greyish, other fins rosy. Rare. Pl.9.

Fam. Aulopidae

Eyes large, mouth extended below them; large 1st dorsal, 2nd dorsal rudimentary; fins with free ray tops.

62. **Aulopus filamentosus** (Bloch.) Aulopus filamentosus (GB,GD-113,GL-62). M. *Żumbrell.* Żumbrell (GD-113). E. Mediterranean flagfin. 30-40cm. +. Olive green with spots of various shades, underside pinkish; a dark spot usually on operculum and a large spot before 1st dorsal in female; fins reddish with yellow spots and darker blotches on caudal and dorsal. rare. Pl.9.

Fam. Synodontidae

Head frog-like, with eyes above mouth cleft; numerous teeth; 2nd dorsal rudimentary.

63. **Synodus saurus** (Linn.) Salmo saurus (GT); Saurus lacerta (GR,GAVG-17); Saurus griseus (GD-112,GL-61); Synodus saurus (JB). M. *Skalm.* Skalm (GT,GR,GAVG-17,GD-112,GL-61,JB); Gremxula tal-baħar, Sawru (GL-61). E. Atlantic lizardfish. 30-40cm. +. Greyish, greenish, olive or ochre with irregular faint markings; underside pale. Small specimens with about 10 very faint vertical bands on the sides. Frequent close to shore, deeper waters. Pl.9.

Fam. Chlorophthalmidae

Eyes large, mouth cleft extended to middle of eye outline, and forward projecting beyond upper snout; teeth very tiny but numerous; 2nd dorsal rudimentary.

64. **Chlorophthalmus agassizi** Bon. Chlorophthalmus agassizi (JB). M. *Panjol.* Panjol (JB). E. Shortnose greeneye. 20-40cm. Iris of eye green; body yellowish brown ochre with some markings; lateral band dark. Rare. A bottom fish, but apparently occasionally taken with others. Pl.9.

Fam. Myctophidae

Body laterally flattened, with very large eyes. Mouth cleft reaches behind eye margin; 2nd dorsal rudimentary.

65. **Electrona rissoi** (Cocco) Scopelus rissoi (GL-60), 5-8cm. Brownish black back, down to silvery sides; scales and eyes large; many luminous points on body. A deep-water seafisah which apparently comes close to surface by night and occasionally taken with other fishes. Very rare. Pl.9.

Fam. Paralepididae

Body very elongated, flattened laterally; dorsal on 2nd half of body length;

2nd dorsal rudimentary; anal highest. Rudimentary fin between anus and anal: 66; snout elongated, no rudimentary fin between anus and anal: 67; pectorals long, reaching to pelvics, no rudimentary fin between anus and anal: 68.

66. **Lestidiops sphyrenoides** (Riss) Paralepis sphyrenoides (GD-114,GL-63). 10-26cm. Back dark brownish or greyish white, abdomen silvery, flanks often pinkish, fins pale; scales absent, except on lateral line. Deep water; sometimes taken with others. Rare. Pl.9.

67. **Paralepis coregonoides** Riss. Paralepis coregonoides (GIOG-6); Paralepis cuvieri (GD-115,GL-64). 20-30cm. Generally brownish silvery with purplish reflections, pale underside. Deep water; rare; sometimes taken with others. Pl.9.

68. **Sudis hyalina** Raf. Paralepis hyalina (GD-116,GL-65). 50-85cm.+. Greyish silvery, tinted pinkish, abdomen pale. Deep water; rare. Pl.9.

Fam. Anguillidae

Snake-like, lower jaw longer than snout; scales concealed; eyes small; elongated dorsal and anal continuous with tail; dorsal starts mid-back length; no pelvics.

69. **Anguilla anguilla** (Linn.) Muraena anguilla (GT), Anguilla vulgaris (GR,GB,GD-63); Anguilla anguilla (GAVG-4,GL-66,JB). M. *Sallura*. Sallura (GT,GR,GAVG-4,GB,GD-63,GL-66,JB). E. Eel. 40-90cm. Blackish-greyish, generally dark but variable. Can live in all types of water, including sea, brackish, and watercourses if close to sea; often found in wells placed there to eliminate other micro-organisms. Frequent in muddy inlets. Pl.9.

Fam. Muraenidae

Snake-like, with anterior body elevated or humped; scales absent; pectorals and pelvics absent; dorsal originates from behind neck and is continuous with caudal and anal.

70. **Gymnothorax unicolor** (Del.) Muraena unicolor (GR,GAVG-3,GB,GD-73,GL-76). M. *Morina kannella*. Morina (GR,GAVG-3). E. Brown moray. 60-80cm.+. Uniformly dark brown or reddish brown; fins with pale edges. Not common. Sometimes considered to be a form of the following species. Pl.10.

71. **Muraena helena** Linn. Muraena helena (GT,GR,GAVG-2,GB,GD-72, GL-75,JB). M. *Morina*. Murina (GT,GL-75); Marina (GL-75); Morina (GR,GAVG-2,GB,GD-72, GL-75,JB). E. Mediterranean moray.

1.00-1.20m. Variable, blackish brown with golden yellow markings or vice versa, often marked with white. Frequent on rocky and weedy bottoms, mostly nocturnal. Pl.10.

Fam. Nettastomidae

Scales absent; upper jaw longer than the lower; teeth numerous; no pelvics or pectorals; dorsal and anal continuous with caudal.

72. **Nettastoma melanurum** Raf. Nettastoma melanurum (GD-67,GL-74). M. *Papra*. Papra (GD-67,GL-74). E. Blackfin sorcerer. 50-80cm. Brownish or dark ochre, often tinged reddish; lighter underside; fins partly edged blackish. Deep water. Occasionally taken. Pl.10.

Fam. Congridae

Snake-like; pectorals present; dorsal starts after pectorals. Eyes large, head snake-like, dorsal starts mid-pectorals length: 73; eyes small, head elevated, dorsal starts after pectoral tips: 74.

73. **Arisoma balearicum** Del. Conger balearicus (GR,GAVG-7,GB); Congermuraena balearica (GD-65,GL-68); Arisoma balearicum (VJ). M. *Morina falza*. Serp il-baħar (GR); Serp (GAVG-7,GD-65); Morina falza (VJ). E. Balearic conger. 20-50cm. Variable, but dark yellowish ochre-light brownish body, often greenish yellow and with reddish-brown markings; lips reddish, fins margined dark. Sometimes considered young of conger. Deep water, rather rare. Pl.10.
74. **Conger conger** Linn. Muraena conger (GT); Conger niger (GAVG-5,GB); Conger verus (GAVG-6); Conger vulgaris (GB); Helmichthys punctatus (GIOG-3); Conger conger (GD-64,GL-67,JB). M. *Gringu*. Gringu (GT,GD-64,GL-67); Gringu ta' barra (GAVG-5,GB, GD-64,GL-67); Gringu tal-port (GR,GAVG-6,GB,GD-64,GL-67); Gringu abjad (GB,GD-64,GL-67); Gringu iswed (GB,GL-67); Gringu tal-blat, Ringu (GL-67). E. Mediterranean conger (/Conger eel). 1.0-2.5m+. Dark, greyish; variable; lateral line whitish; fins bordered black. Common. Pl.10.

Fam. Ophichthidae

Body very snake-like; scales absent, pectorals absent. Upper snout much longer than lower jaw, eye small: 75; no pectoral or caudal fins, dorsal and anal extremely shallow, upper snout just longer than lower jaw, eyes small: 76; upper snout shortly projects over lower jaw, eyes large, dorsal and anals fins quite developed, pectorals present, dorsal starts just after pectorals: 77; upper snout projects slightly over lower jaw, eyes average size, dorsal and anal quite developed, pectorals present, dorsal originates far from pectorals: 78; upper snout just projects over lower jaw, eyes small, dorsal and anal quite developed, pectorals present, dorsal originates just a little after the pectorals; 79.

75. **Apterichthus caecus** (Linn.) Sphagebranchus caecus (GD-71,GL-73). M. *Gringu bla ġwienaħ*. E. European finless eel. 30-60cm. Yellowish to light brown, sometimes reddish or pinkish, underside lighter. Rare. Pl.10.

76. **Dalophis imberbis** (Del.) Sphagebranchus imberbis (GD-70,GL-72). M. *Gringu serp*. E. Armless snake eel. 1.0-1.50m. Bluish, pinkish, purplish grey back, or entirely yellowish; pale underside with variable refelctions, sometimes with small, dark or white spots; dorsal edge pale. Rare. Pl.10.

77. **Echelus myrus** (Linn.) Conger myrus (GB); Myrus vulgaris (GD-66,GL-69); Echelus myrus (JB). M. *Gringu tar-ramel*. Gringu tan-nemex (GB,GD-66); Gringu tat-tikek (GL-69); Gringu tar-ramel (JB,GL-69). E. Bluntsnout snake eel. 40-90cm. Brownish, yellowish; unpaired fins posteriorly darker. Rare. Sometimes considered as a form of the common conger. Pl.10.

78. **Ophichthus rufus** (Raf.) Ophichthus hispanus (GD-69,GL-71). M. *Serp il-baħar ħalqu qasir*. Serp il-baħar (GD-69,GL-71). E. Rufus snake eel. 50-60cm. Yellowish, brownish, entirely pale. Very rare. Pl.11.

79. **Ophisurus serpens** (Linn.) Ophisurus serpens (GT,GAVG-p10,GB,GD-68,GL-70,JB,VJ). M. *Serp il-baħar ħalqu twil*. Serp il-baħar (GT,GB,GD-68,GL-70,VJ); Serp (JB). E. Longjaw snake eel (/Serpent eel). 1.50-2.30m+. Golden brown with reddish tints above, pale below; fins bordered dark, often marked with dark spots. Rare, in mud and sand. Pl.11.

Fam. Belonidae

Body very slender, jaws also very slender and elongated, the lower slightly longer than the upper, but the young may have a shorter lower jaw; pelvics far back in 2nd half of the body; anal and dorsal uninterrupted, continuous. Dorsal does not reach close to the tail: 80; dorsal reaches very close to the tail: 81.

80. **Belone belone** (Linn.) Esox belone (GT); Belone rostratus (GR); Belone acus (GAVG-22); Belone vulgaris (GD-106); Belone belone JB,GL-78);

Belone belone gracilis (VJ). M. *Imsella*. Imsella (GT,GR,GAVG-22,GD-106,GL-78,JB); Imsella komuni (VJ). E. Garfish. 50-80cm. Back dark greenish blue, sides and underside silvery white, rosy close to head; variable. Mediterranean species belongs to ssp. gracilis. Frequent close to coast. Pl.11.

81. **Tylosurus acus** Lac. Tetrapterus orphie (GT), Belone imperialis (GD-107, GL-79); Tylosurus acus imperialis (VJ). M. *Imsella imperjali*. Imsella imperjali (GT.GD-107,GL-79,VJ). E. Agujon needlefish. 80-90cm.+. Dark bluish green, abdomen silvery; dorsal black, pectoral brown; tail base blackish. The Mediterranean species belongs to the ssp. imperialis. Sometimes considered a form of the preceding. Frequent. Pl.11.

Fam. Scomberesocidae

Body not as slender as in the Belonidae; jaws pointed, the lower longer than the upper; dorsal and anal interrupted, terminating in separate finlets.

82. **Scomberesox saurus** (Walb.) Scomberesox camperii (GR,GAVG-20,JB); Scomberesox saurus (GD-108,GL-77,JB). M. *Kastardella*. Kastardella (GR,GAVG-20,GD-108,GL-77,JB); Kristadella (GL-77). E. Atlantic saury. 20-45cm. blue-black greyish above, silvery white underside; fins bluish or pinkish. Not frequent, but sometimes offshore shoals can be encountered leaping at the surface. Pl.11.

Fam. Exocoetidae

Body very smooth and streamlined, pectorals very elongated, wing-like; ventrals long. Dorsal with 12-14 rays, anal 8-10 rays: 83; dorsal 10-12 rays, anal 11-13 rays: 84.

83. **Cheilopogon heterurus** (Raf.) Exocoetus evolans (GT,GL-80); Exocoetus exsiliens (GR,GAVG-21,GD-109); Exocoetus volitans (GD-110,GL-81). M. *Rondinella komuni*. Rondinella (GT,GR,GAVG-21,GD-110,GL-80,81); Rundinella (GL-80,81). E. Flying fish. 20-30cm. Dark, bluish black above, silvery white below; fins greyish. Previous records in local lists of E.evolans, E.exsiliens and E.volitans should be attributed to this species, since this is well known in central and westernm Mediterranean, but the others are only stragglers. Specimens examined have hitherto belonged to C. heterurus. Pl.11.

84. **Hirundichthys rondeletii**(Val.) Exocoetus rondeleti (GD-111,GL-82);

Cypselurus rondeleti (JB). M. *Rondinella rara*. Rondinella (GD-111,GL-82); Rundinella (GL-82). E. Flying fish. 23-25cm. Back dark bluish black, silvery white below; fins tinged brownish. Uncommon, but occasionally observed. Pl.11.

Fam. Cyprinodontidae

Anal opposed to the single dorsal; mouth short, deflected upwards; tail unforked.

85. **Aphanius fasciatus** Nardo. Micromugil timidus (GR,GAVG-18); Micromugil macrogaster (GR); Cyprinodon calaritanus (GD-100,GL-52,GJ-p25). M. *Bużaqq*. Bużaqq (GR,GAVG-18,GD-100, GL-52). E. Killifish. 5-6cm (males), 6-7cm (females). Yellowish, greyish greenish; males with 8-13 broad, vertical, dark bands from back to abdomen; body lighter in females, bands thinner, shorter, lighter, confined to the sides. Used to be frequent in brackish water, but now declining and endangered. It is an endemic subspecies. Pl.12 a)male),b)female).

Fam. Macroramphosidae

Snout very narrow and elongated out of a laterally compressed, oval body; 1st dorsal far back, long, spiny.

86. **Macroramphosus scolopax** (Linn.) Centriscus scolopax (GT,GR,GAVG-137); Macroramphosus scolopax (GD-121,GL-83,JB). M. *Bekkaċċa tal-baħar*. Bekkaċċa (GAVG-137,GD-121,GL-83); Trumbetta (GL-83); Bekkaċċa tal-baħar (GR); Pixxitrumbetta (JB). E. Snipefish (/Trumpetfish, Bellowsfish). 10-15cm. Reddish pink back, lighter below; smaller specimens silvery white. Not common; often in small groups close to bottom. Pl.12.

Fam. Syngnathidae

Thin, weak, elongated body covered with hard plates, with a tiny mouth at the end of an elongated snout; males with a brood pouch. Head bent down, snout short: 87; head bent down, snout long: 88; no pectoral, caudal or anal fins, body elevation thickened to 3 times that of heads: 89; no pectoral, caudal or anal fins, body elevation equal to or slightly higher than that of head: 90; anal and pectoral present; 10 rays on caudal; dorsal midway of body length, shallower than body height: 91; anal and pectorals present; 10 rays on caudal; dorsal midway of body length and as high as body: 92;

anal and pectorals present; 10 rays on caudal; dorsal on front half of body, which is more slender than hind half: 93; anal and pectoral fins present; 10 rays on caudal fin; dorsal on front half of body which is thicker than the hind half: 94; anal and pectorals present, 10 rays on caudal, dorsal at middle or slightly on hind half of body: 95.

87. **Hippocampus hippocampus** (Linn.) Sygnatus hippocampus (GT); Hippocampus brevirostris (GR,GAVG-157,GD-50,GL-84). M. *Żiemel tal-baħar ħalqu qasir.* Żiemel (GT); Żiemel tal-baħar (GR,GAVG-157,GD-50,GL-84). E. Short-nosed seahorse. 10-15cm. Greyish or brownish often with irregular paler markings. Frequent weedy bottoms, but not easy to detect. Pl.12.

88. **Hippocampus ramulosus** Leach. Hippocampus guttulatus (GR,GAVG-158,GD-51,GL-88,JB). M. *Żiemel tal-baħar ħalqu twil.* Żiemel tal-baħar (GAVG-158,GD-51,GL-88); Żiemel (JB). E. Long-nosed seahorse. 13-16cm. Variable, ranging yellowish to dark reddish brown, with white or light blue tiny spots over body; often with projections on head and dorsal body. Not frequent. Pl.12.

89. **Nerophis maculatus** Raf. Nerophis maculatus (GD-58,GL-91). M. *Gremxula tal-baħar ħamra.* E. Red-banded pipefish. 20-30cm. Brownish reddish greenish; males with pale spots along back, females with dark spots; sides with thin, red, vertical bands. Not frequent. Pl.12.

90. **Nerophis ophidion** (Linn.) Nerophis ophidion (GD-57,GL-90). M. *Gremxula tal-baħar irqiqa.* Gremxula tal-baħar (GD-57,GL-90). E. Straight-nosed pipefish. 20-30cm. Brownish olive green, pale underside; females may have blue markings on underside. Frequent weedy bottoms; often confused with its congeners. Pl.12.

91. **Syngnathus acus** Linn. Syngnathus acus (GT,GD-52,GL-86,JB); Syngnathus rubescens (GD-54,GL-87). M. *Gremxula tal-baħar ħoxna.* Gremxula tal-baħar (GT,GL-86,87); Gremxula (JB). E. Great pipefish. 30-40cm.+. Greenish olive, reddish brown, underside lighter; some darker patches on sides. Frequent on weedy bottoms. Pl.12.

92. **Syngnathus abaster** Riss. M. *Gremxula tal-baħar ħalqha qasir.* 15-20cm. Greenish, olive, brownish marked darker on the sides. Not frequent on weedy bottoms; in some areas replaces similar species.

93. **Syngnathus phlegon** Riss. Syngnathus pelagicus (GD-55,GL-89). M. *Gremxula tal-baħar kaħla.* 15-20cm. Body blue, underside pale silvery, normally with blue markings on sides. Syngnathus pelagicus Osb., of previous lists may have been a reference to this species. Rare, weedy bottoms.

94. **Syngnathus tenuirostris** Ratk. Syngnathus tenuirostris (GD-53,GL-88). M. Gremxula tal-baħar. (GD-53,GL-88). Records refering to this species are probably a misidentification and refer to some form of Syngnathus typhle Linn.

95. **Syngnathus typhle** Linn. Siphostoma typhle (GR,GD,GL-92); Syngnathus typhle (GAVG-159). M. *Gremxula tal-baħar ħalqha għoli*. Dremxula tal-baħar (GR,GAVG-159); Gremxula tal-baħar (GD,GL-92). E. Deepnosed pipefish. 30-35cm. Green olive brownish, irregularly marked with lighter patches, lines or white dots. Frequent, sometimes common. Pl.12.

Fam. Gasterosteidae

96. **Gasterosteus aculeatus** Linn., E. Three-spined stickleback.
Note:- Listed by GAVG-85, is not within this area, and should not form part of our fauna.

Fam. Macrouridae

Eyes very large; body anteriorly massive, and posteriorly ending in a point; long 2nd dorsal and anal continuous with the minute caudal.

NOTE: **Coelorhynchus coelorhynchus** (Riss.) E. Blackspot grenadier listed by JB as M. Ġurdien tal-fond (JB), and **Hymenocephalus italicus**, E. Italian grenadier, also listed by JB as M. Ġurdien (JB), are both deep water fish. Although in the area, they are difficult to encounter or examine, and need further investigation.

Fam. Merlucciidae

1st dorsal over origin of pectorals, 2nd dorsal just behind 1st and runs close to tail.

97. **Merluccius merluccius** (Linn.) Gadus merluccius GT); Merluccius esculentus (GR,GAVG-52); Merluccius merluccius (GD83,GL-98,JB) M. *Marlozz*. Marlozz (GT,GR,GAVG-52, GD-83, GL-98); Maroz (GR); Merluzz (JB); Merluzz ewropew (VJ) Mirluzz (GL-98). E. Hake 35-70cm.+. Head elongated, level with the back, lower jaw protruding, longer than the upper snout. Back grey, fading down to white underside. Frequent. Pl.12.

Fam. Gadidae

Usually with a rudimentary or conspicuous barbel on lower jaw. 3 dorsals and 2 anals:98 to 100; 2 dorsals 1 anal: 101 to 105; 1st anal below 2nd dorsal, eyes very large: 98; 1st anal below 1st and 2nd dorsal, extending far beyond the latter close to origin of 3rd: 99; 1st anal below 2nd doprsal, eyes average size: 100; first dorsal extremely shallow, 2 barbels on upper snout, one on lower jaw: 101; 1st dorsal extremely shallow, 2 barbels on upper snout, one on lower jaw: 102; pelvics short: 103; pelvics long, reaching beyond anal origin: 104; pelvics long, just reaching the anal: 105.

98. **Gadiculus argenteus** Guich. Gadus argentatus (GD-80,GL-95); Gadiculus argentatus (JB). M. *Nemusa*. Nemusa (GD-80,GL-95,JB). E. Silvery pout. 8-10cm.+. Body silvery with rosy reflections with some dark spots. Deeper waters; not frequent. Pl.12.

99. **Micromesistius poutassou** (Riss.) Merlangus vernalis, Merlangus medlycotti (GR); Gadus poutassou (GD-79,GL-94); Micromesistius poutassou (JB). M. *Stokkafixx*. Marlozz, Marluzz (GL-94); Stokkafixx (JB,GL-94,VJ); Putassu (VJ). E. Blue whiting. 20-30cm.+. Back brownish dark grey with bluish tinge, fading to silvery and white underside. Deep water; rare. Pl.13.

NOTE: **Pollachius pollachius** (Linn.) E. Pollack, and Pollachius virens (Linn.), E. Saith, are both listed by JB, as M. Bakkaljaw, but they are both outside the Mediterranean. the Maltese name is applicable to Trisopterus minutus (Linn.).

100. **Trisopterus minutus** (Linn.) Gadus blennoides (GT,GD-78,GL-93); Gadus(Trisopterus)capelanus (JB). M. *Bakkaljaw*. Bakkaljaw (GD-78,GL-93); Mankana (JB,GL-93). E. Poor cod. 12-20cm. Ochre brown back fading down through light reddish brown to silvery underside, often with small dark spots all over the body. Occasionally frequent, especially juveniles in shallow water. Pl.13.

101. **Gaidropsarus mediterraneus** (Linn.) Gadus mustela (GT); Motella mustela (GR,GAVG-55); Onos fuscus (GD-87,GL-103);Onos maculatus (GD-88,GL-104). M. *Ballottra tal-baħar*. Ballottra (GT,GR,GAVG-55,GD-87,88,GL-103); Ballottra tat-tikek (GL-104). E. Shore rockling. 20-25cm. Reddish or blackish brown upperside, paler underside, with or without patches. Rather rare.

NOTE: **Gadus mustela** Linn., listed by GT is not in the area, and can be assumed to refer to Gaidropsarus mediterraneus (Linn.) Onos maculatus (GD-88) is considered synonymous with this, but may have been refering to some form of the following species.

102. **Gaidropsarus vulgaris** (Cloq.) Onos tricirratus (GD-89,GL-105,JB). M. *Ballottra tat-tikek*. Ballottra (GD-89,GL-105,JB); Ballottra tal-fond, Pixxilupu (GL-105); Ballottra tat-tikek (VJ). E. Three-bearded rockling.

35-42cm. Dark brown, orange or reddish brown, light ochre below; head, sides, back, dorsal and caudal fins spotted and marked dark brown. Occasioanally met with on rocky, weedy bottoms. Pl.13.

103. **Molva dipterygia** (Penn.) Molva elongata (GD-86,GL-102); Molva molva (JB); Molva macrophthalmus (JB). M. *Linarda*. Lipp (JB,GL-102); Linarda (GL-102). E. Blue ling. 0.80-1.3m. Back reddish brown, posteriorly often with small, black spots. Rather rare. Pl.13.

104. **Phycis blennoides** (Brunn.) Phycis tinca (GR,GAVG-54); Urophycis blennoides (GD-84); Phycis blennoides (JB,GL-100). M. *Lipp abjad*. Lipp (GR,GAVG-54); Lipp abjad (GD-84,GL-100,JB); Lupu (GL-100). E. Greater forkbeard. 13-40cm.+. Silvery, dark greyish brown, paler below; fins edged blackish. Rare. Pl.13.

105. **Phycis phycis** (Linn.) Blennius phycis (GT); Phycis blennoides (GR); Phycis mediterranea (GR,GAVG-53); Uraleptus mediterranea (GD-55); Phycis phycis (JB,GL-101). M. *Lipp tal-qawwi*. Lipp (GT,GD-85,GL-101); Bakkaljaw tal-ħama (GR); Lipp tal-qawwi (JB,GL-101); Lupu (GL-101). E. Forkbeard. 20-50cm.+. Dark brownish or black on back, fading to lighter underside; 1st dorsal brownish, other fins bordered white. Occasional. Pl.13.

Fam. Moridae

2 dorsals, the 1st very shallow, the 2nd very long and uniform, anal 1, but may appear divided into 2.

106. **Mora moro** (Riss.) Mora mediterranea (GD-82,GL-97). M. *Marlozz tal-fond*. 50-60cm Variable; brownish black with purple reflections, greyish white below with silvery reflections. Deep water; occasional.

NOTE:**Gadella maraldi** (Riss.) recorded as Uraleptus maraldi Riss. (GL-99), on closer examination should be attributed to a form of Phycis phycis (Linn.).

Fam. Regalecidae

Body long, laterally flattened with relatively small head, elevated dorsal region; dorsal fin as long as body, anal absent; pelvics long and thread-like.

107. **Regalecius glesne** Asc. M. *Fjamma tal-fond*. E. Oarfish. 2.50-5m.+. Body whitish silvery with some dark streaks; fins red, head tinged with blue. Deep sea fish, ocasionally reported as sighted in open sea. Was shown head of a specimen in 1966, St. Paul's Bay. Very rare. Pl.13.

Fam. Trachypteridae

Body laterally compressed, high head profile, posteriorly tapering to fan-shaped caudal; dorsal as long as long as body. Head height about 1/10 body length: 108; head height about 1/5 body length: 109.

108. **Trachypterus trachypterus** (Gmel.) Trachypterus taenia (GB); Trachypterus iris (GD-215,GL-107);Trachypterus trachypterus (JB). M. *Fjamma*. Pixxi fjamma (GB); (Fjamma GD-215,GL-107,JB); Żigarella (VJ). E. Ribbonfish (/Dealfish). 1.0-1.5m. Very variable with age, but silvery white body, dorsal fin red, a few long dark spots on sides of back. Occasionally met with. Pl.14.

109. **Zu cristatus** (Bon.) Trachypterus spinolae (GB); Trachypterus cristatus (GD-216,GL-108). M. *Fjamma rasha kbira*. E. Scalloped ribbon fish. 0.30-1.00m. Body silvery white with some vertical, dark, irregular bands; Tail fin dark. Sometimes thought to be a form of Trachypterus trachypterus (Gmel.), but has persistent characteristics. Frequent. Pl.14.

Fam. Lophotidae

Body laterally flat, elevated, dorsal whole body length, with first rays compact projecting as high as head or higher.

110. **Lophotus lacepedei** Giorn. Trachypterus iris (GR);Gymnetrus cepedianus (GAVG-136); Lophotes cepedianus (GD-214,GL-106). M. *Fjamma tal-qarn*. Fjamma (GR,GAVG-136,GD-214,GL-106); Xabla (GR); Fjamma tal-qarn (VJ). E. Crested oarfish (/Unicorn fish). 1.0-1.50m. Back blue, fading to whitish underside, with some light silvery white spots; fins rosy. Rare. Pl.14.

Fam. Trachichthydae

Body short, high, laterally compressed, lower jaw bent upwards.

111. **Hoplostethus mediterraneus** Cuv. Hoplostethus mediterraneus (GAVG-84,GL-109,JB). M. *Ġurdien tal-warda*. Ġurdien tal-warda (JB,GL-109). E. Rosy soldier fish. 15-20cm. Body rosy, reddish or pinkish with silvery or purplish reflections and some brown spots. Rare. Pl.14.

Fam. Zeidae

Body short, laterally extremely compressed, profile very high; head occupied a whole third of the body, mouth large, lower jaw greatly upturned.

112. **Zeus faber** Linn. Zeus faber (GT,GR,GAVG-133,GB,GD-239, GL-110,JB); Zeus pungio (GL-111). M. *Pixxi San Pietru*. Pixxi San Pietru (GT,GR, GAVG-133, GB,GD-239,GL-110); Moxt (GR,GAVG-133,GL-110); San Pietru, Ħuta San Pietru (GL-110). E. John Dory. 20-50cm. Grey with yellow and silvery reflections, with a characteristic, large, round blackish spot circled golden yellow on each side. Zeus pungio Cuv. & Val.(GL-111), with a robust, elongated bone behind the eye and fainter spot, formerly thought as diferent, is considered as a form. Frequent. Pl.14.

Fam. Caproidae

As Zeidae, but eyes relatively very large, snout pointed, mouth very small.

113. **Capros aper** (Linn.) Capros aper (GR,GAVG-134,GB,GD-240, GL-112,JB). M. *Pixxi trumbetta*. Pixxi trumbetta (GR,GB, GD-240,GL-112); Bassas (GD-240,GL-112); Minfaħ (JB,GL-112); Trumbetta (GL-112). E. Boarfish. 5-12cm. Yellowish, often pinkish or reddish, with or without small, vertical bands; abdomen silvery. Not frequent. Pl.14.

Fam. Serranidae

Dorsal, anal, ventral fins with spines followed by rays; ventral with 1 spine and 5 rays; operculum with a few spines near posterior margin. Caudal with elongated tips, 3rd dorsal spine very long: 114; caudal with elongated tips, dorsal rays more than twice as long as dorsal spines: 115; caudal outline convex, dorsal 10 or 11 spines: 116; caudal outline straight, usually concave, dorsal with 11 spines: 117; caudal outline straight or slightly convex, dorsal with 11 spines: 118; caudal outline convex, dorsal with 11 spines: 119; caudal outline straight, dorsal 11 spines, anal 11 or 12 rays after spines: 120; caudal outline convex, dorsal 11 spines: 121; caudal outline straight or slightly concave, dorsal 10 spines: 122; caudal outline straight or slightly convex, dorsal 10 spines: 123; caudal outline straight or slightly concave, dorsal 10 spines: 124.

114. **Anthias anthias** (Linn.) Labrus anthias (GT); Anthias sacer (GR,GAVG-70,GD-209,GL-127); Anthias anthias (VJ). M. *Pixxiroża tar-rigi*. Pixxiroża (GT,GR,GAVG-70,GD-209,GL-127,VJ); Pixxiroża ħotbija (VJ). E. Swallowtail sea perch. 15-20cm. Pinkish, reddish, with or without dark, hazy markings, with 3 longitudinal yellow bands on head. Frequent. Pl.14.

115. **Callanthias ruber** (Raf.) Callanthias peloritanus (GD-208,GL-126); Callanthias ruber (VJ). M. *Pixxiroża ta' l-għajn*. Pixxiroża (GD-208,GL-126); Pixxiroża ta' l-għajn (VJ). E. Parrot sea perch. 15-20cm. Body reddish, pinkish, fading down to yellowish white abdomen; fins yellowish. Frequent. Pl.14.

116. **Epinephelus aeneus** (Geoff.S.H.) Epinephelus aeneus (GD-204,GL-122). M. *Dott tal-faxxi*. Fellusa taċ-cerna (GD-204,GL-122). E. White grouper. 0.80-1.00m. Brownish olive grey with a few, more or less longitudinal pale bands behind the eye, and a few nearly vertical, dark stripes and scattered spots. Sometimes confused with the young of Epinephelus gauza (Linn.). Frequent. Pl.15.

117. **Epinephelus alexandrinus** (Val.) Epinephelus alexandrinus (GD-205,GL-123); Epinephelus chrysotaenia (GD-206,GL-124). M. *Dott tat-tebgħa safra*. Dott (GD-205,206,GL-123,124); Dott tat-tebgħa safra (VJ). E. Golden grouper. 45-80cm.+. Brownish purplish grey with a golden lateral patch when living; immature specimens sepia brown with several, dark, longitudinal lines. Not common. Adult and juvenile were formerly thought to be different species. Pl.15.

118. **Epinephelus caninus** (Val.) Sparus addottus (GT), Epinephelus caninus (GD-203,GL-121). M. *Dott abjad*. Dott abjad (GT,GD-203,GL-121); Dott iswed (GT). E. Dogtooth grouper. 1.0-1.50m. Grey with purplish tinge with a few darker bands radiating behind the eye in younger specimens. Not frequent. Pl.15.

119. **Epinephelus gauza** (Linn.) Perca gygas (GT); Ċerna gigas (GR,GAVG-71);Epinephelus gigas (GD-202,GL-119). M. *Ċerna*. Ċerna (GT,GR,GAVG-71,GD-202,GL-119); Manann (GL-119). E. Dusky grouper. 1.0-1.50m. Dark purplish brown irregularly marked with lighter blotches and spots; caudal edged white. Frequent. Pl.15.

120. **Mycteroperca rubra** (Bloch) Epinephelus acutirostris (GD-201,GL-120). M. *Ċerna denbha dritt*. Ċerna (GD-201,GL-120). E. Comb grouper. 50-80cm. Purplish brown, with irregular, pale patches and streaks, especially in juveniles. Rocky places; not frequent. Pl.15.

121. **Polyprion americanus** (Schn.) Polyprion cernium (GT, GR, GAVG-72, GD-194, GL-115); Epinephelus sicanus (GD-207, GL-125); Polyprion americanus (JB). M. *Ħanżir tal-fond*. Ħanżir (GT, GAVG-72, GL-115); Ħanżir tal-qiegħ (GR); Ħanżir tal-fond (GD-194, GL-115); Dott (GD-194, JB); Ċerna, Ċerna tal-fond, Dott tal-fond, Mananni (GL-115); Ħanżir taċ-ċimi (VJ). E. Wreckfish (/Stonebass). 1.0-1.50m.+. Brownish grey, with hazy patches especially in the

younger specimens; fins darker. In some areas frequent. Pl.15.

122. **Serranus cabrilla** (Linn.) Perca cabrilla (GT);Serranus cabrilla (GR, GAVG-68, GD-199, GL-118, JB, VJ). M. *Sirran*. Serran (GT, GL-118; Kanna (GT, GL-118) Sirran (GR, GAVG-68, GD-199, GL-118); Sirrana (JB); Sirrana tar-rigi (VJ). E. Comber. 20-30cm. +. Ochre pinkish with some deep yellow bands on sides of head, and several brownish vertical stripes on the sides. Frequent, rocky, weedy bottoms. Pl.16.

123. **Serranus hepatus** (Linn.) Serranus hepatus (GR, GAVG-69, GD-198, GL-116); Paracentropristis hepatus (JB). M. *Ħanżir burqax*. Ħanżir burqax (GR); Ħanżir żgħir (GR); Ħanżir (GAVG-69, GD-198, GL-116); Sirrana tar-ramel (JB, GL-116); Burqax tax-xewka (GL-116); Ħanżir tal-hofor (VJ). E. Brown comber. 10-13cm. +. Greenish reddish brown with about some dark vertical stripes on sides, some yellowish, ochrish bands on head, and distinguished by a black patch in the middle of the dorsal fin. Frequent. Pl.16.

124. **Serranus scriba** (Linn.) Perca scriba (GT); Serranus scriba (GR, GAVG-67, GD-200, GL-117, JB). M. *Burqax*. Burqaxa (GT); Burqax (GR, GAVG-67, GD-200, GL-117, JB); Sirena (GL-117). E. Painted comber. 20-28cm. +. Ochre yellowish brownish with some lateral, vertical, broad bands, brownish abdominal blotch, with blue and pale reddish lines resembling scribbles writing on the cheeks; small red spots are scattered on the fins. Frequent. Pl.16.

Fam. Moronidae

2 dorsals, 1 anal, 2nd dorsal with 1 spine before rays, anal 3 spines before rays. Dorsals with a short distance between them: 125; dorsals with hardly any distance between them: 126.

125. **Dicentrarchus labrax** (Linn.) Perca labrax (GT); Labrax lupus (GR, GAVG-65); Dicentrarchus labrax (GD-196, GL-114, JB). M. *Spnotta*. Spnotta (GT, GR, GAVG-65, GD-196, GL-114); Spina, Spigola, Lupu (GL-114). E. European seabass. Dark bluish green with silvery sheen; abdomen silvery; juveniles with dark spots. Specimens with a black spot on the back edge of operculum and spotted body, were formerly thought to be this species, and should be attributed to Dicentrarchus punctatus Bloch. Frequent. Pl.16.

126. **Dicentrarchus punctatus** (Bloch.) Dicentrarchus punctatus (JB, VJ). M. *Spnotta tat-tbajja*. Spnotta tat-tbajja (JB, VJ). E. Spotted seabass. 40-50cm. +. Bluish green with silvery sheen with a black blotch on edge of operculum and blackish spots dispersed over the sides. Formerly

thought to be a juvenile form of Dicentrarchus labrax (Linn.). Frequent. Pl.16.

Fam. Apogonidae

Eyes very large, 1st dorsal all spiny, 2nd dorsal with 1 spine before rays; anal with 2 spines before rays.

127. **Apogon imberbis** (Linn.) Mullus imberbis (GT); Apogon rex mullorum (GR, GAVG-66); Apogon imberbis (GD-195, GL-113, JB). M. *Sultan iċ-ċawl*. Sultan iċ-ċawl (GT, GR, GAVG-66, GD-195, GL-113, JB); Ċawla ħamra (GL-113). E. Cardinal fish. 9-13cm.+. Body brownish, abdomen silvery lighter and silvery; fins reddish, a few dark spots grouped at base of tail. Often frequent on rocky shores. Pl.16.

Fam. Cepolidae

Body very elongated and laterally compressed; dorsal long, from nape to tail, anal also long, starting slightly after pelvics; eyes large.

128. **Cepola rubescens** Linn. Cepola taenia (GT); Cepola rubescens (GR, GAVG-135, GB, GD-213, GL-215, JB); Cepola macrophthalmus (VJ). M. *Fjamma ħamra*. Fjamma (GT, GR, GAVG-135, GD-213, GL-215); Xabla (GR); Pixxifjamma (GB); Fjamma ħamra (JB, VJ). E. Red bandfish 25-40cm.+. Body and fins orange red or yellowish, underside lighter; dorsal sometimes with a red spot. Occasional. Pl.16.

Fam. Pomatomidae

2 dorsals, closely associated; 1st dorsal; shallow, 2nd elevated; anal preceded by 2 short spines.

129. **Pomatomus saltator** (Linn.) Temnodon saltator (GB, GD-235, GL-139); Pomatomus saltator (JB, VJ). M. *Serra tas-snien*. Serra tas-snien (JB, GL-139, VJ); Serraġsirra imperjali (GL-139). E. Bluefish. 40-70cm.+. Greenish dark with silvery sheen, abdomen light; base of pectorals dark. Rare. Pl.17.

Fam. Carangidae

2 dorsals; 1st short, often rudimentary; 2nd dorsal preceded by a spine; anal preceded by 2, usually obvious spines (except in Alectis); caudal ends in 2 pointed lobes; pectorals and pelvics with 1 spine beofre rays; body laterally compressed and very elevated; fins of young with very elongated

first filaments. 1 dorsal and 1 anal, none preceded by obvious spines, but finrays very elevated: 130; 1st dorsal represented by very shallow spines, mouth reches to posterior eye margin: 131; 1st dorsal shorter than 2nd, posterior lateral line straight with prominent harsh projections: 132; 1st dorsal higher than 2nd, the hind level part of the lateral line thick, and originating before middle of the 2nd dorsal: 133; 1st dorsal represented by shallow spines, mouth reaches beyond posterior eye margin: 134; 1st dorsal hardly represented by spines, mouth reaches anterior eye margin and pupil: 135; 1st dorsal higher than 2nd, straight posterior part of lateral line thick, short, originating after middle of 2nd dorsal: 136; 1st dorsal closely reaches height of 2nd: 137; 1st dorsal represented by 6 shallow spines, mouth reaches anterior eye margin: 138; 1st dorsal higher than 2nd, lateral line all with thick scales, its straight posterior half, much thicker: 139; 1st dorsal higher than 2nd, lateral line all with thick scales, all about same thickness, its straight part starts far beyond tip of pectorals: 140; 1st dorsal higher than 2nd., lateral line all with thick scales, all about the same thickness, its straight part starts at tip of pectorals: 141.

130. **Alectis alexandrinus** (E.Geoff.S.H.) Caranx alexandrinus (GD-238, GL-134). E. Alexandria pampano. 40-60cm.+. Bluish silvery. Rare.

131. **Campogramma glaycos** (Lac.) Lichia vadigo (GR, GAVG-116, GD-233, GL-138). M. *Serra.* Stillera (GR); Sirra (GAVG-116, GD-233, GL-138); Serra, Karraba, Ċervjola (GL-138). E. Vadigo. 45-60cm. Dark greyish green, down to sides projecting into short bands over white of abdomen; sides often pinkish. Sometimes confused with young of Seriola dumerili Riss.; used to be rare, now often frequent. Pl.17.

132. **Caranx crysos** (Mitch.) Caranx fusus (JB). M. *Sawrella imperjali denbha iswed.* Sawrella imperjali (JB). E. Blue runner. 30-50cm.+. Dark or light greenish blue or ochrish greenish, fading into golden silvery grey on sides and underside. Often confused with Seriola dumerili Riss. Frequent. Pl.17.

NOTE: Alepes djedaba (Forsk.) Caranx kalla Tort. (JB), M. *Sawrella imperjali ċatta.*(JB), E. Shrimp scad, 20-30cm.+. Dark or light greenish blue or ochrish green, fading into silvery grey with golden reflections on sides and paler on underside. Very similar to the preceding, but with more prominent projections on the level posterior portion of the lateral line; a blackish blotch present on the operculum. Often confused with the young of Seriola dumerili Riss. It is an eastern Mediterranean fish migrating from the Red Sea, and now becoming quite frequent.

133. **Caranx rhonchus** E.Geoff.S.H. Decapterus rhonchus (JB); Caranx

rhonchus (VJ). M. *Sawrella imperjali tat-tikka sewda.* Sawrella imperjali (JB, VJ). E. False scad. 30-50cm.+. Greenish brown back, down to paler and white ventrally, with or without an ochre longitudinal line on the sides; characteristic large black spot on 2nd dorsal, and a small one on the posterior margin of operculum. Occasionally frequent. Pl.17.

134. **Lichia amia** (Linn.) Lichia amia (GB, GD-232, GL-137, JB, VJ). M. *Serra ħoxna.* Sirra (GB, GD-232, GL-137); Serra (JB, GL-137); Ċervjola (GL-137); Serra ħoxna (VJ). E. Leerfish. 0.60-1.0m.+. Bluish greenish blackish brown back, down to paler or whitish ventrally; fins with black tips; smaller specimens may have some dark stripes. Frequent. Pl.17.

135. **Naucrates ductor** (Linn.) Scomber ductor (GT); Naucrates fanfanus (GR, GAVG-115b, GB); Naucrates ductor (GR, GAVG-115a, GB, GD-230, GL-135, JB). M. *Fanfru.* Fanfru (GT, GR, GABVG-115a, GB, GD-230, GL-135, JB). E. Pilotfish. 30-40cm.+. Bluish black back down to pale underside; 5 or 6 vertical, broad, blackish stripes on silvery sides; caudal tips pale. Frequent. Sometimes follows ships. Pl.17.

136. **Pseudocaranx dentex** (Bl.& Sch.) Trachurus imperialis (GT); Selenia luna (GR); Caranx luna (GR, GAVG-120, GD-238, GL-133); Caranx dentex (GB). M. *Sawrella imperjali.* Sawrella imperjala (GT, GR, GAVG-120); Sawrella imperjali (GB, GD-238, GL-133). E. Guelly jack. 30-40cm.+. Greenish blue back to silvery white ventrally; hind edge of operculum marked black. Not frequent. Pl.18.

137. **Seriola dumerili** (Riss.) Scomber acciola (GT); Trachurus alicolus (GT); Mycropterix dumerili (GR, GAVG-118, GB); Seriola dumerili (GD-234, GL-140, JB). M. *Aċċola.*(adult), *Ċervjola.*(young). Aċċola (GT, GR, GAVG-118, GB, GD-234, GL-140, JB); Ċervjola (GR, GAVG-118, GB, GD-234, GL-140); Serra (GT); Serjola (GL-140). E. Greater amberjack. 0, 80-1.0m.+. Bluish or brownish green back with silvery or pinkish grey underside; young paler, often with some lateral, vertical bands. Frequent. Pl.18.

138. **Trachinotus ovatus** (Linn.) Scomber amia (GT); Lichia glaucus (GR); Centronotus glaucus (GB, GD-231, GL-136); Trachynotus glaucus (JB). M. *Strilja.* Stillira (GT); Sirra (GR); Stillera (GAVG-117, GB, GD-231, GL-136); Strilja (JB, GL-136); Ċervjola imperjali (GL-136). E. Derbio (/Pompano). 25-40cm.+. .Dark bluish green back, down to silvery sides and underside, with indistinct vertical grey stripes or blotches; dorsal, anal and caudals tipped black. Frequent. Pl.18.

139. **Trachurus mediterraneus** (Steind.) Trachurus mediterraneus

(GD-237, GL-132, JB); Trachurus mediterraneus mediterraneus (VJ). M. *Sawrella għajnejh kbar*. Sawrella (GD-237, GL-132, JB); Sawrella kaħla (GL-132); Sawrella tal-ħama (VJ). E. Mediterranean horse mackerel. 25-35cm. +. Back dark blue with greenish tinge fading to paler silvery sides and underside. By some considered a form of Trachurus trachurus L. Frequent. Pl.18.

140. **Trachurus picturatus** (Bowd.) Trachurus picturatus (VJ). M. *Sawrella kaħla*. Sawrella kaħla (VJ). E. Blue jack mackerel. 30-40cm. +. Dark bluish greenish back down to silvery white sides and underside; a dark spot on hind edge of operculum. Occasionally frequent.

141. **Trachurus trachurus** (Linn.) Scomber trachurus (GT); Caranx trachurus (GR, GAVG-119); Trachurus trachurus (GB, GD-236, GL-131, JB, VJ). M. *Sawrella komuni*. Sawrella (GT, GR, GAVG-119, GB, GD-236, GL-131); Sawrella kaħla (JB, GL-131); Sawrella bajda, Sawrella ċatta (VJ). E. Atlantic horse mackerel. 25-40cm. +. Back dark greenish blue down to paler silvery sides and abdomen; a small spot on hind edge of operculum. Common. Pl.18.

Fam. Coryphaenidae

Body laterally compressed, head profile with very elevated forehead in adults. shallow in juveniles; one dorsal fin from head to tail; scales relatively tiny. Anal half the length of and as high as the dorsal: 142; anal about 2/3 height of dorsal, and about half its height: 143.

142. **Coryphaena equiselis** Linn. Coryphaena equisetis (GD-243, GL-130). M. *Lampuka rara*. Lampuka (GD-243, GL-130). E. Pompano dolphin fish. 40-60cm. +. Back greenish or silvery grey, sides and underside silvery; dark spots scattered over body; caudal clear edges and not merely the tips as in young of Coryphaena hippurus L.; fins greyish. Rare. Some consider it to be the young of C.hippurus L.

143 **Coryphaena hippurus** Linn. Coryphaena hippurus (GT, GR, GAVG-121, GB, GD-242, GL-129, JB); Coryphaena pelagica (GR, GAVG-122, GB). M. *Lampuka*. Lampuka (GT, GR, GAVG-121, 122, GB, GD-242, GL-129, JB). E. Common dolphin fish. 0, 50-1.0m. +. Blackish greenish blue back, down to silvery sides and underside with golden sheen and small dark spots. Caudal tips clear in the young, pelvics dark. C. equiselis L. often considered by some to be a juvenile form of this species. Forms an important fishery. Apparently becoming less frequent, and specimens offered for sale are much smaller. May be on the decline through overfishing, and may be on the way of the tunny fishery which has been discontinued. Pl.18.

Fam. Bramidae

Body very elevated and laterally compressed; head profile rounded, bulky, mouth cleft nearly vertical, eys and scales large, 1 high dorsal, 1 anal, both anteriorly elevated.

144. **Brama brama** (Bonn.) Brama raji (GB, GD-246, GL-128, JB, VJ). M. *Pixxiluna.* Pixxiluna (GB, GD-246, GL-128, JB); Ċawlun (VJ). E. Ray's bream. 35-50cm. +. Blackish body with silvery reflections; pectorals, pelvics and tips of caudal light grey. Occasional. Pl.19.

Fam. Sciaenidae

Single dorsal, but may appear as two, because of a wedge space between spiny anterior and soft posterior. Dorsal profile shallow but convex, body height a quarter of body length: 145; dorsal profile very prominently convex, body height nearly half body length: 146; dorsal profile very prominently convex, body height about a third of body length: 147.

145. **Argyrosomus regius** (Asso) Sciaena aquila (GD-210, GL-141). M. *Gurbell.* Gurbell rar (GD-210, GL-141); Gurbell, Ombra (GL-141). E. Meagre. 45-60cm. +. Greyish, greenish silvery back, silvery sides with greenish yellow reflections; fins pale pink or brownish. rare. Pl. 19.

146. **Sciaena umbra** Linn. Scoena umbra (GT, JB); Corvina nigra (GR, GD-211, GL-142, JB). M. *Gurbell tork.* Gurbell (GT, GR, GL-142); Għarab, Tork (GD-211, GL-142); Għarbi (GL-142); Gurbell tork JB, GL-142). E. Brown meagre. 20-40cm. +. Dark brown and grey back with silvery yellow sides and abdomen; pelvics, anal, lower caudal and edge of 2nd dorsal black. Rather rare. Pl.19.

147. **Umbrina cirrosa** (Linn.) Umbrina cirrosa (GR, GAVG-86, GD-212, GL-143, JB, VJ). M. *Gurbell tad-daqna.* Gurbell rar (GR); Gurbell (GAVG-86, GD-212, GL-143, JB); Gurbell tal-qawwi (VJ); Umbrina, korvina, Lumbrina, Ombrina (GL-143). E. Bearded umbrina 30-45cm. +. Dark silvery, greyish or brownish back, some longitudinal lines on upper sides; operculum edged blackish. Occasionally frequent. Pl.19.

Fam. Mullidae

Body laterally compressed with high head profile; 2 barbels on lower jaw; 2 dorsals, well separated. Barbels shorter than pectorals, forehead profile angle very elevated: 148; barbels longer than pectorals, forehead profile angle not very elevated: 149;

148. **Mullus barbatus** Linn. Mullus barbatus (GT, GR, GAVG-73, GD-180, GL-178, JB). M. *Trilja bla faxxi*. Trilja ħamra (GT); Trilja bla faxxi (GR); Trilja (GAVG-73,GD-180, GL-178); Trill, Trilja żgħira (GL-178). E. Red Mullet. 12-18cm.+. Back reddish pink, sides pink, underside lighter and silvery; body without yellow stripes or markings. Frequent. Pl.19.

149. **Mullus surmuletus** Linn. Mullus surmuletus (GT, GR, GAVG-74, GD-179, GL-177, JB, BB). M. *Trija tal-faxxi*. Trilja tal-faxxi (GT); Trilja tal-faxxi sofor (GR); Trilja (GAVG-74, GD-179, GL-177); Trilja tal-qawwi (JB, GL-177); Trill (Gl-177). E. Striped red mullet. 20-30cm.+. Fairly common. Pl.19.

NOTE: **Pseudopeneus barberinus** Lac.(JC), M. *Trilja ta' Lvant*, E. Goatfish, 40-50cm.+, is similar to the other red mullets, with pinkish body, but has a characteristic longitudinal dark stripe on each side from mouth to end of 2nd dorsal, and a dark spot on tail base. Apparently spreading from eastern Mediterranean. Frequent.

Fam. Sparidae

Body laterally compressed, dorsal outline prominently convex, especially anteriorly; one long dorsal, spiny anteriorly and with soft rays posteriorly; pelvics with one spine preceding rays; anal with 3 spines preceding rays; caudal prominent, terminating in two points; hermaphrodite, with either the female (protogynous) first or the male (protandrous) developing. Body length X4 height, eyes large: 150; body length about X3 height: 151; body length about X3 height, 2nd and 3rd dorsal spines very elongated into filaments: 152; body lenmgth X2 1/2 height: 153; body length X2 height: 154; body length X2 height: 155; body length X2 1/2 height: 156; body length X2 height: 157; body length nearly X2 1/2 height: 158; body length nearly X3 height: 159; body length X3 height: 160; body length over X3 height: 161; body length nearly X3 height: 162; body nearly X3 height: 163; body length X2 height: 164; body length nearly 2 1/2 height: 165; body length nearly X3 height: 166; body nearly X3 height: 167; body length X2 1/2 height: 168.

150. **Boops boops** (Linn.) Sparus boops (GT); Boops vulgaris (Gr, GAVG-g4); Box boops (GD-176, GL-176); Boops boops (JB). M. *Vopa*. Vopa (GT, GR, GAVG-84, GD-176, GL-176, JB). E. Bogue. 15-30cm.+. Bluish green back down to silvery-golden sides, with a few thin longitudinal yellow-golden bands; base of pectorals with a black spot. Common. Pl.19.

151. **Dentex dentex** (Linn.) Sparus dentex (GT); Dentex vulgaris (GR,

GAVG-98, GD-158, GL-164); Dentex dentex (JB, VJ). M. *Denċi komuni*. Dentiċi (GT, GR, GAVG-98, GD-158, GL-164, JB); Denċi (GD-158, GL-164); Spnotta komuni (VJ); Denċi komuni (VJ). E. Common dentex. 40-55cm. +. Dark greenish greyish blue back, and pinkish with hazy dots, lighter and silvery underside; juveniles lighter with spots more distinct; pectorals may be darker at the base. Frequent. Pl.20.

152. **Dentex gibbosus** (Raf.) Dentex gibbosus (GD-159, GL-165, VJ). M. *Denċi ħotbi*. Denċi ħotbi (VJ); Dentiċi, Denċi (GD-159, GL-165). E. Pink dentex. 40-50cm +. Body silvery pink with tiny black spots, caudal edged blackish, and some dark at the base of pectorals and behind operculum. Some consider it a form of Dentex dentex L. Not common. Pl.20.

153. **Dentex macrophthalmus** (Bloch,) Dentex macrophthalmus (JB, VJ). M. *denċi ta' l-għajn*. denċi ta' l-għajn (JB, VJ). E. Large-eyed dentex. 20-40cm. +. Body reddish pink with fore base of dorsal, edge of anal and lower caudal lobe clear. Occasional.

154. **Diplodus annularis** (Linn.) Sparus annularis (GT); Sargus annularis (GR, GAVG-89, GD-171, GL-158); Diplodus annularis (JB, VJ). M. *Sparlu*. Sparlu (GT, GR, GAVG-89, GD-171, GL-158, JB); Sparlu tan-nejba (VJ). E. Annular sea bream. 10-20cm. +. Ochre silvery grey with vertical black bands in the young; fins clear, pelvics yellow; there is a black band at tail base, close to caudal. Frequent in bays and harbours. Pl.20.

155. **Diplodus cervinus** (Low.) Sargus fasciatus (GD-175, GL-160); Diplodus cervinus (GL-302); Diplodus trifasciatus (JB). M. *Sargu imperjali*. Sargu imperjal (GD-175, GL-160); Sargu skur (JB). E.Zebra sea bream. 30-30cm. +. Body shiny grey with five broad, blackish brown vertical bands on sides; between and below eyes blackish, as is a spot at base of pectorals; dorsal, anal, caudal edged dark. Not frequent. The Mediterranean species belongs to the ssp. cervinus. Pl.20.

156. **Diplodus puntazzo** (Cetti) Sparus puntazzo (GT); Charanx puntazzo (GR, GAVG-90, GD-170); Puntazzo puntazzo (GL-161, JB). M. *Mogħża*. Mogħża (GT, GR, GAVG-90, GD-170, GL-161, JB); Muzo lungo, Pizzutu (GL-161). E. Sharpsnout sea bream. 20-30cm. +. Silvery body with 11 to 13 dark and light alternating verticl bands from back to sides; base of pectorals, tail, and with edge of dorsal, caudal and anal black. Frequent. Pl.20.

157. **Diplodus sargus** (Linn.) Sparus sargus (GT);Sargus rondeleti (GR, GAVG-88, GD-173); Sargus vetula (GD-174, GL-159); Sargus sargus

(GL-156); Diplodus sargus (JB). M. *Sargu komuni*. Sargu (GT, GAVG-88, GD-173, GL-156, JB); Xirgħien (GR). E. White sea bream. 25-30cm. +. Body silvery, with 7-9 vertical, narrow bands from back to sides, alternating dark and light; a small dark spot at base of pectorals and a larger one on each side of tail base. Frequent rocky shores, bays and harbours. Pl.20.

158. **Diplodus vulgaris** Geoff.S.H.) Sparus salviani (GT); Sargus salviani (GR, GAVG-87); Sargus vulgaris (GD-172, GL-157); Diplodus vulgaris (JB). M. *Xirgħien*. Xirgħien (GT, GR, GAVG-87, GD-172, GL-157, JB); Sargu (GL-157). E. Common two-banded sea bream. 20-30cm. +. Greyish body with blackish area behind head before dorsal, tail base, caudal edge and upper base of pectorals. Frequent. Pl.20.

159. **Lithognathus mormyrus** (Linn.) Sparus mormyrus (GT); Pagellus mormyrus (GR, GAVG-93, GD-169, GL-171); Lithognathus mormyrus (JB). M. *Mingus*. Mingus (GT, GR, GAVG-93, GD-169, GL-171, JB); Minkus, Ajula (GL-171). E. Striped sea bream. 20-30cm. +. Silvery body, lighter underside, 13-15 dark vertical bands from back to sides, often very slightly alternating light and dark; blackish brown forehead and eye region, as are the dorsal and caudal fins. Frequent. Pl.21.

160. **Oblada melanura** (Linn.) Sparus melanurus (GT), Oblada melanura (GR, GAVG-102, GD-178, GL-174, JB). M. *Kaħlija*. Kaħlija (GT, GR, GAVG-102, GD-178, GL-174, JB). E. Saddled bream. 15-25cm. +. Silvery body, with thin, longitudinal lines on sides, back dark grey down to lighter abdomen; Caudal base with black blotch on each side. Frequent. Pl.21.

161. **Pagellus acarne** (Riss.) Pagellus acarne (GR, GAVG-94, GD-166, GL-170, JB, VJ). M. *Bażuga*. Bażuga (GR, GAVG-94, GD-166, GL-170, JB); Paġella bastarda (GL-170); Bażuga bajda (VJ). E. Axillary sea bream. 20-30cm. +. Greyish with pinkish reflections, forehead region darker grey, abdomen light silvery; base of pectorals with a red blotch, fins often edged grey. Occasionally frequent. Pl.21.

162. **Pagellus bogaraveo** (Brunn.) Sparus bogaraveo (GT); Pagellus bogaraveo (GR, GAVG-95, GD-167, GL-173, JB); Pagellus centrodontus (GR, GAVG-96, GD-168, GL-169, JB). M. *Bażuga kaħla*. Bażuga (GT, GR, GAVG-95, GD-167, GL-173, 169); Paġella (GD-168, GL-169, 173); Paġella kaħlija (GL-173); Moppa (GL-169); Paġella tal-garġi (JB, GL-169);Bażuga kaħlija (JB, VJ); Bażuga tal-qasir (for the young)(VJ). E. Red sea bream. 20-40cm. +. Pinkish grey body with a red blotch behind operculum above pectoral base; head and fin tips usually denser pink. Frequent. PL.21.

163. **Pagellus erythrinus** (Linn.) Sparus erythrinus (GT); Pagellus erythrinus (GR, GAVG-97, GD-165, GL-172, JB, VJ). M. *Paġella.* Paġella (GT, GR, GAVG-97, GD-165, GL-172); Paġella ħamra (JB, VJ). E. Pandora. 20-30cm.+. Body pink abdomen lighter with very small scattered blue spots; deeper pink opercular edge and base of pectoral. On being alarmed or caught, temporary red lines appear. Frequent. Pl.21.

164. **Pagrus auriga** (Val.) M. *Paġru ħamrani.* E. Red banded sea bream. 20-40cm... Pinkish grey with silvery reflections, with characteristic, dark, purplish red vertical bands from back down to sides, alternating broad and thin, starting with the broadest below anterior spines of dorsal. Apparently uncommon; caught Xghira area, San Anard.(J.Farrugia, J. Ellul, Zabbar, Oct.1977). Pl.21.

NOTE: Also recorded, (JB, VJ) **Pagrus coerulostrictus** (Val.) as Pagrus ohrenbergi VAl.(JB); Sparus ohrenbergi Val.(VJ). M. *Paġru rar.* (JB, VJ), E. Blue spotted sea bream. 25-45cm.+. Silvery body with pinkish tinge spotted blue, often with greyish patches in larger specimens; blackish at the base of dorsal and caudal edge; underside paler. Occasionally frequent in rocky places.

165. **Pagrus pagrus** (Linn.) Sparus hurta (GT); Sparus pagrus (GT); Pagrus orphus (GR, GAVG-92, GD-164, GL-168); Pagrus vulgaris GR, GAVG-91, GD-163); Pagrus pagrus (JB, GL-167); Sparus sparus (VJ). M. *Paġru.* Paġru (old specimens) (GT, GR, GAVG-91, GD-163, GL-167, 168); Ħawwad (young specimens) (GD, GR, GAVG-92, GD-164, GL-167, 168). E. Common sea bream. 30-40cm.+. Pinkish body, head and caudal denser; often with tiny blue spots in young specimens. Frequent. Pl.22.

166. **Sarpa salpa** (Linn.) Sparus salpa (GT); Boops salpa (GR, GAVG-100); Box salpa (GD-177, GL-175, JB). M. *Xilpa.* Xilpa (for sdults) (GT, GAVG-100, GD-177, GL-175); Ġwiela (for young) (GT, GAVG-100, GD-177, GL-175); Tartarella (for very young) (GAVG-100, GD-177, GL-175); Sarpa (GL-175.) E. Salema. 25-35cm +. Body bluish light silvery grey with thin, golden, longitudinal lines on sides with a blackish dot at pectoral base. Frequent shoals close inshore. Pl.22.

167. **Sparus aurata** Linn. Sparus aurata (GT, JB); Chrysophrys aurarta (GR, GAVG-103, GD-162, GL-166). M. *Awrata.* Awrata (GT, GR, GAVG-103, GD-162, GL-166); Orata, Dorata, denċi awrata (GL-166). E. Gilthead sea bream. 30-40cm.+. Body silvery with a black blotch on operculum, a gold stripe between the eyes, black along middle of dorsal and edge of caudal; sides may have golden yellow sheen, with

irregular, serrated, longitudinal lines. Frequent. Pl.22.

168. **Spondyliosoma cantharus** (Linn.) Sparus cantharus (GT); Cantharus orbicularis (GR, GAVG-101, GD-161); Cantharus lineatus (GD-170); Spondyliosoma cantharus (GL-162, JB); Spondyliosoma orbicularis (GL-163). M. *Tannuta*. Tannuta (GT, GR, GAVG-101, GD-160, 161, GL-162, 163, JB); Tanuda (GL-162, 163), Kantaru (GL-163). E. Black sea bream. 25-35cm. +. Body silvery, with variable greenish blue and pinkish reflections, often with yellowish, irregular, longitudinal streaks especially in young; balckish or bluish forehead and dorsal and caudal margin. When alarmed, may show temporary vertical broad bands on sides. Frequent. Pl.22.

Fam, Centracanthidae

One long dorsal, caudal with 2 points. Eye diameter occupies about 1/2 head height, dorsal depressed at the middle: 169; eye diameter occupies less than 1/2 head height, dorsal higher than anal: 170; eye diameter occupes 1/3 head height, dorsal about as high as anal, body length about X3 height:171; eye diameter (male) occupies about 1/3 head height, female about 1/2, dorsal about as high as anal, female dorsal slightly higher than anal, body length more than X4 height: 172.

169. **Centracanthus cirrus** Raf. Smaris insidiator (GIOG-7, GD-253, GL-207). M. *Arżnella rara*. Arznella rara (GIOG-7, GD-153, GL-207). E. Plain picarel. 10-15cm. +. Body silvery pink without dark blotches, lighter underside. Rare. Apparently confused with other Smaris species. Pl.22.

170. **Spicara flexuosa** Raf. Smaris chryselis (GR, GAVG-104, GD-150, GL-206). M. *Arżnell*. (male), *Munqara*. (female). Arżnell (GR, GAVG-104, GD-150, GL-206); Munqara (GR, GAVG-104, GD-150, GL-206). E. Small-spot picarel. 10-15cm. +. Body ochrish grey with golden reflections and scattered, indistinct grey markings which fade after death; a small distinct black blotch on each side; underside paler. Males more robust. Common. Pl.22.

171. **Spicara maena** (Linn.) Sparus maena (GT);Maena vomerina (GR-105, GD-157, GL-212); Maena osbekii (GR, GAVG-106); Maena vulgaris (GD-154, GL-209); Maena zebra GD-155, GL-210); Maena jusculum (GD-156, GL-211); Maena maena (JB). M. *Arżnella tat-tikek*. Xurrafa (GT, GD-154, 155, GL-209, 210) Minnula (GT); Pajżan (GT, GD-157); Arżnella bastarda (GR, GAVG-105); Mirli (GR, GD-154, GL-209, JB); Pizzintun (GR); Ċawla, Menula (GL-209). E. Blotched picarel. 18-22cm. Body silvery blue, rarely brownish, with silvery sides, small scattered grey spots, and a conspicuous, black,

longitudinally oval blotch on each side, sometimes faded. Males more robust. Often confused with its congeners because of its variability in colour and sexual differences. Frequent. Pl.23.

172. **Smaris smaris** (Linn.) Sparus smaris (GT); Sparus polynimus (GT); Smaris alcedo (GD-149, GL-204); Smaris vulgaris (GD-151, GL-205); Smaris mauri (GD-152, GL-208); Maena smaris (JB). M. *munqara*.(female), *Arżnell(a)*.(male). (GT, GD-149, 151, GL-204, 205); Munqara bastarda (GT); Arżnella (GD-149, 151, GL-204, 205, JB). E. Piċarel. 10-16CM. +. Silvery grey body, with a characteristic blackish spot on each side above the pectoral tips; lighter underside. Males more robust, with some bluish markings. Fairly common close inshore. Confused with its congeners because of its variablity. Pl.23a (male), b (female).

Fam. Pomacentridae

Body laterally compressed, upper and lower profiles nearly identical, mouth small, single dorsal, with the rays behind the spines being higher.

173. **Chromis chromis** (Linn.) Sparus chromis (GT); Heliastes chromis (GR, GD-148, GL-203); Chromis castanea (GAVG-25); Chromis chromis (JB, BB). M. *Ċawla*. Ċawla (GT, GR, GAVG-25, GD-148, GL-203, JB); Kastanjola (GL-203). E. Damsel fish. 7-11cm. +. Body blackish brown with golden reflections, appearing striped dark longitudinally because of a pale area on each scale; caudal margin pale; younger specimens with single fins edged blue and blue bands on the body; younger specimens appearing in August are bright luminous blue. Common close inshore. Pl.23 a (young), b (adult).

Fam. Labridae

Body langth at least about X3 height, dorsal single over the whole back, with 12-19 spines followed by rays, except in Coris, Thalassoma, Xyrichthys which have 8-10 spines; lips soft, very obvious and well developed; caudal straight or obtuse; anal with 3 spines preceding rays, except Acantholabrus with more. Extremely variable, and sometimes difficult to determine, due to sexual dimorphism, age, and sex reversal in several species, besides colour variation within the same species. Body length and height ratios given here are approximate, and exclude caudal and other fins. Other distinguishing factors are to be found in the colour descriptions. Anal 4-6 spines, snout profile very acute, body length over X3 height: 174; Dorsal spines up to 10, sex reversal female to male, body length over X4 height: 175; body length over X4 height, snout profile very acute: 176; body length over X3 height: 177; body length over X4 height, head profile very elongated: 178; body length over X4 height, snout profile very acute: 179; body length over X3 height: 180; body length over X3 height, head very elongatged: 181; body length over X3 height: 182, 183; body length less than X3 height, sex reversal: 184; body length over X3 height: 185; body length less than X3 height: 186; body length over X3 height, head and snout very elongated: 187; body length less than X3 height, sex reversal: 188; dorsal spines 8, body length less than X4 height: 189; dorsal spines up to 10, forehead very elevated, body length X3 height, sex reversal: 190.

174. **Acantholabrus palloni** (Riss.) Acantholabrus palloni (GL-197). M. *Tirda rara*. E. Scale-rayed wrasse. 15-20cm.+. Variable; brownish green, brownish yellow or reddish brown, reddish purple with paler underside; dark blotch on hind dorsal and above tail. Close to shore, but rarely taken. Pl.23.

175. **Coris julis** (Linn.) Labrus julis (GT); Julis mediterraneus (GR) Julis geofredi (GR, GAVG-45, GD-144, GL-199); Julis vulgaris GAVG-44, GD-143); Coris julis (JB, GL-198, BB). M. *Għarusa*. Għarusa (GT, GR, GAVG-44, GD-143, GL-198, JB); Għarusa armla (GR, GD-144, GL-199); Pixxiré (GL-198). E. Rainbow wrasse. 14-22cm.+. Variable with depth and sex. Females rather small and dull coloured, reddish brown above, whitish below and a pale band along sides; males larger with bright colours, a broad, wavy, orange-red longitudinal band on sides and a black and orange or red spot on front of dorsal; whole body with some bluish, greenish patches and markings. Frequent close to shore. Pl.23 a(male), b(female).

176. **Labrus bimaculatus** Linn. Labrus trimaculatus (GT, JB); Labrus mixtus (GT, GR, GAVG-41, GL-182); Labrus carneus (GR, GAVG-43); Labrus bimaculatus (GD-134, VJ). M. *Parpanjol*. Parpanjol (GT, GR, GAVG-41, GD-134, GL-182, JB); Bagħal (GT, GR, GAVG-43, GD-134, GL-182); Tirda kaħla (GL-182); Maskarat (VJ). E. Cuckoo wrasse. 20-30cm.+. Variable; males blue head and shoulders, the rest bright orange yellow; green markings around the head, green markings and streaks on the rest of the body and fin edges; females reddish or orange yellow with large, dark spots along base of dorsal to tail, alternating with whitish spots. Frequent. Pl.24 a(male), b(female).

177. **Labrus merula** Linn. Labrus merula (GT, GR, GAVG-40, GD-133, GL-180, JB). M. *Mirli*. Għarab (GT); Mirli (GR, GAVG-40, GL-180); Tirda (GD-133, GL-180) Merli (JB); Merla (GL-180). E. Brown wrasse. 25-40cm.+. Body brownish, especially in younger specimens,

to greenish, blue or purplish with some pale blue spots; fins edged blue, underside lighter. Very variable. Frequent. Pl.23.

178. **Labrus viridis** Linn. Labrus turdus (GT, GR, GAVG-42, GD-131, JB); Labrus festivus (GR, GAVG-39, GD-132, GL-181); Labrus viridis (GL-179). M. *Tirda*. Murlin aħdar (GT); Tirda tal-lok (GT); Boxbox (GR, GAVG-39, GD-132, GL-181); Tirda (GR, GAVG-42, GD-131, GL-179, 181, JB). E. Green wrasse. 30-40cm.+. Body green, underside lighter often with silvery reflections or golden in the larger specimens, and with a longitudinal pale line on each side; there may also be golden spots scattered regularly on the sides; fins marked with colourd blotches. Common, also inshore. Pl.24,

NOTE: **Labrus bergylta** Asc., recorded by JB as M. Morlin (JB), does not appear to occur in the Mediterranean.

179. **Lapponella fasciata** (Cocco) Crenilabrus iris (GR); Ctenolabrus iris (GAVG-48, GD-142, GL-196). M. *Debba*. Debba (GR, GAVG-48, GD-142). 10-12cm.+. body reddish or pinkish with a dark line from eye to pectoral base; dark spot usually present in middle and base of caudal and on dorsal. Often frequent in deep water. Pl.24.

180. **Symphodus cinereus** (Bonn.) Labrus fuscus (GT); Crenilabrus cinereus (GD-139, GL-188); Synphodus cinereus (VJ). M. *Tirda griża*. Tirda tax-xaħma (GT); Tirda griża (VJ). 8-12cm+. Variable; body greyish or greenish brown or rosy brown, yellowish green, usually marked paler or darker; beginning of dorsal and base of caudal with a black spot; males lightly coloured with blue streaks on head region. Rare. Pl.24.

181. **Symphodus doderleini** Jord. Crenilabrus serranus, Crenilabrus zeraphinus, Crenilabrus schembrianus, Crenilabrus dubius, Crenilabrus inrtermedius, Crenilabrus locaninus (GR, GAVG-27, 28, 34, 36); Crenilabrus doderleini (GD-140, GL-191). M. *Tirda tar-rig abjad*. Tirda (GR, GAVG-30). Extremely variable, giving rise to several new descriptions by GR, GAVG; brown or reddish brown, yellow or orange yellow, paler undrside; two longitudinal dark lines and a wide, white stripe along sides, and a small black spot on the tail base. Occasional in bays and harbours. Pl.24.

182. **Symphodus mediterraneus** (Linn.) Crenilabrus brunnichi (GR); Crenilabrus mediterraneus (GD-136, GL-184, JB, VJ); Crenilabrus chrysophorus (GR). M. *Boxbox*. Boxbox (GR, GD-136, GL-184, VJ); Tirda (GR); Buxiħ (GL-184, JB). E. Axillary wrasse. 10-14cm.+. Extremely variable, due to sex, age, spawning time etc... Males greenish, brownish, greyish, bluish, reddish, with rows of small, pale

spots; base of pectoral with a large, blue blotch circled yellowish, and an uncircled one at tail base; females pale, browsh ochre, marked with dark blotches, with a large, brown blotch circled yellowish at pectoral base and an uncircled one at tail base. Frequent close inshore. Pl.25 a(male), b(spawning season male), c(female).

183. **Symphodus melanocercus** (Riss) Crenilabrus melanocercus (GL-190, VJ). M. *Tirda denbha iswed.* Tirda ta' denbha iswed (VJ). E. Black tailed wrasse. 10-13cm.+. Males yellowish, reddish, grey or fawn, with blue spots and blotches, elongated patch about the eyes and lower jaw, more colourful during mating season; caudal black edged and based whitish; females yellowish, brownish, reddish, caudal edged white, based yellow. Not common. Pl.25 a(male), b(female).

184. **Symphodus melops** (Linn.) Crenilabrus melops (GL-189). M. *Tirda rasha ħamra.* E. Corkwing. 14-25cm.+. Very variable; back brownish, reddish, greyish with rows of spots and 4 or 5 spots on dorsal; vertical or indistinct bands on sides sometimes absent, fins variously marked; a characteristic, black-brown, bent, elongated spot behind eye. Close inshore; not frequent. Pl.25 a(male), & Pl.26 b(female).

185. **Symphodus ocellatus** Forsk. Labrus ocellatus (GT); Labrus olivaceus (GT); Crenilabrus ocellatus (GR, GAVG-29, GD-137, GL-183, JB); Labrus guttatus (GT). M. *Tirda tal-warda.* Murlin imnikket (GT); Tirda tat-trexx (GT); Tirda tal-warda (GT, GD-137, GL-183); Tirda (GR, GAVG-29); Tirda ta' l-għajn (GL-183). E. Rose cheeked wrasse. 6-9cm.+. Very variable. A dark blotch on operculum, mostly reddish, and a black spot at caudal base; males greenish or brownish orange with other colours about the eyes and head; females brownish yellow with 2 or 3 longitudinal dark bands on back and sides. Frequent. Pl.26a(male), b(female).

186. **Symphodus roissali** (Riss.) Crenilabrus roissali (GR, GAVG-32, GD-138, GL-187); Symphodus roissali (VJ). M. *Boxbox kannella.* Boxbox (GAVG-32, GD-138, GL-187); Tirda ħadra (VJ). E. Pink lipped wrasse. 8-15cm.+. A most variable species. Males brown, with reddish or green sheen, with many indistinct, yellow, green and brown markings and pink lips; females brown and often greenish brown; both sexes with a black spot at caudal base, hazy, broad, longitudinal bands and scattered spots. Frequent. Pl.26 a(male), b(female).

187. **Symphodus rostratus** (Bloch) Labrus turdus (GT);Coricus rostratus (GR, GD-141, GL-195); Coricus virescens (GAVG-47). M. *Buxiħ aħdar.* Buxiħ (GT, GL-195); Buxiħ aħdar (GR, GAVG-47, GD-141, GL-195); Tirda (GL-195). E. Long-snouted wrasse. 8-12cm.+.

Infinitely variable, brownish, reddish, greyish, green, blotched or marked, sometimes unmarked; more or less characteristic is a yellow or whitish band along mouth to forehead. Frequent. Pl.26.

188. **Symphodus tinca** (Linn.) Crenilabrus propinquus (GR, GAVG-36, GL-186); Crenilabrus geoffroi (GR, GAVG-35); Crenilabrus pavo (GD-135, GL-185); Crenilabrus tinca (JB); Symphodus tinca (VJ). M. *Tirda mirlija*. Tirda (GAVG-35, GD-135); Mirli, Morlizz, Lappun, Morlin (GL-185); Tirda pagun (JB), Tirda tal-passa (VJ). E. Peacock wrasse. 18-25cm.+. Very variable. Background colour a mixture of or separate green, grey, reddish, brown, yellowish, with undefined light bands on back, with red markings in the more colourful males; a blackish patch at base of pectorals and a black spot at caudal base. Common. Pl.27 a(male), b(female).

189. **Thalassoma pavo** (Linn.) Labrus pavo (GT); Labrus judaicus (GT); Chlorychtis pavo (GR); Julis pavo (GR, GD-145, GL-200); Julis turcica (GAVG-46); Thalassoma pavo (JB, BB, VJ). M. *Lhudi*. Lhudi (GT, GR, GAVG-46, GD-145, GL-200, VJ); Tirda tal-passa (GT); Rużan (JB, GL-200); Tork (GL-200); Bulhudi (VJ). E. Ornate wrasse. 16-20cm.+. Body greyish tinged red with slightly oblique vertical lines, alternating grey and yellow, with some metallic tinge;. dorsal blue, caudal edged black marked red and grey, head with blue markings tinged golden green; scales each with a vertical mark. Males appear greenish, head reddish with blue, and a characteristic vertical, blue band behind pectorals. Females less colourful. Frequent close inshore, in holes; small shoals appear close to surface at sunset. Pl.27 a(male), b(female).

190. **Xyrichthys novacula** (Linn.) Coryphaena novacula (GT); Xirichthys cultratus (GR); Xyrichthys novacula (GAVG-49, GD-146, GL-201, JB). M. *Rużetta*. Rużetta (GT, GR, GAVG-49, GD-146, GL-141, JB); Rozetta (GL-201). E. Cleaver wrasse. 15-25cm.+. Body with pinkish reddish background and silvery blotches on sides; males brighter green or red, paler on the underside; females pinkish; scales each vertically marked blue, head with blue irregular lines. Frequent. Pl.27 a(male), b(female).

Fam. Scaridae

Teeth fused, body covered with very large scales, head-snout profile rather rounded, teeth fused.

191. **Sparisoma cretense** (Linn.) Labrus scarus (GT); Scarus creticus (GR, GAVG-50); Scarus cretensis (GD-147, GL-202); Sparisoma cretense

(JB). M. *Marzpan*. Martspan (GT); Martzpan (GR, GAVG-50, GD-147, GL-202, JB); Marzpan, Marżipan (GL-147). E. Parrotfish. 25-35cm.+. Males greyish or purplish brown with small, scattered, white spots; females more colourful with a red body and a dark blotch over the head and pectoral area, and a yellow blotch preceding caudal fin; side with scattered, small, white spots. Frequent. Pl.28.

Fam. Ammodytidae

Very elongated body, a long dorsal originating after tip of pectorals, with a long anal half or less than half dorsal; lower jaw longer than upper snout.

192. **Gymnamodytes cicerelus** (Raf.) Ammodytes cicerellus (GL-214); Gymnammodites cicerelus (JB); Ammodytes tobianus (GD-74, GL-213). M. *Ċiċċirella*. Fjammetta (JB); Ċiċċirella (GD-74, GL-213). E. Mediterranean sand eel. 12-15cm.+. Dark bluish green back and head or ochre-greenish brown, underside paler, with silvery golden reflections. Frequent. Pl.28.

NOTE: **Ammodytes tobianus** L. formerly recorded, (GD-74, GL-213) as M. Ċiċċirella (GD-74, GL-213), is not within the Mediterranean, and should be attributed to Gymnamodites cicerelus Raf.

Fam. Trachinidae

Body laterally compressed, eyes close to the top front of head; 1st dorsal black with only 5-7 poisonous spines, 2nd dorsal long but shorter than the anal; body length to height ratios given here exclude caudal. No spine on eye frame: 193; 2 spines on eye frame, 1st dorsal with 26-29 spines, body length X4 1/2 height: 194; 2 shallow spines on eye frame, 2nd dorsal 29-32 spines, body length X5 1/2 height: 195; 2 shallow spines on eye frame, 2nd dorsal 24-27 spines, body length X4 1/2 height: 196.

193. **Echiichthys vipera** (Cocco) Trachinus vipera (GD-269, GL-218, JB, VJ). M. *Sawt*. Sawt (GD-269, GL-218); Stracna (JB, GL-218) Traċna lixxa (GL-218, VJ); Sawt nanu (VJ). E. Lesser weaver. 10-15cm. Ochrish body with thin, longitudinal bands of small, dark spots; abdomen white. Frequent in sand. Pl.28.

194. **Trachinus araneus** Cuv. Trachinus araneus (GL-221, JB, VJ). M. *Traċna tat-tbajja*. Traċna (GL-221, JB, VJ); Sawt (GL-221); Traċna tat-tbajja (VJ). E. Spotted weever. 20-30cm.+. Ochrish body with dark, lateral markings and patches. Frequent in muddy bottoms. Pl.28.

195. **Trachinus draco** Linn. Trachinus draco (GT, GR, GAVG-62, GD-268, GL-220, JB, VJ). M. *Sawt kbir*. Sawt (GT, GR, GAVG-62,

JB); Tracna (GT, GD-268, GL-220; Sawt kabbari (VJ). E. Greater weever. 20-30cm. +. Body ochrish brown, often greenish brown, with slightly diagonal dark streaks on the sides; underside pale. Frequent. Pl.28.

196. **Trachinus radiatus** Cuv. Trachinus lineatus (GR, GAVG-63, GL-219, JB); Trachinus radiatus (VJ). M. *Tracna tal-fond.* Tracna (GR, GAVG-63, GL-219); Tracna tal-fond (JB, VJ). E. Streaked weever. 20-30cm. +.Ochrish background, densely marked with rounded streaks in rows on the sides; caudal edged dark. Frequent. Pl.28.

NOTE: The statement that this species was not before recorded (GL-219) was inadvertent, and should have appeared in conjuntion with Trachinus araneus L. (GL-221).

Fam. Uranoscopidae

Body not laterally compressed; head rectangular, eyes on top of head, 1st dorsal black and short, caudal convex, jaws opening vertically.

197. **Uranoscopus scaber** Linn. Uranoscopus scaber (GT, GR, GAVG-64, GD-270, GL-217, JB). M. *Żondu.* Żondu (GT, GR, GAVG-64, GD-270, GL-217, JB). E. Stargazer. 15-25cm. +. Dark ochrish back with lighter sides and white underside; 1st dorsal black. Frequent on muddy and sandy bottoms. Pl. 28.

Fam. Siganidae

Body laterally compressed; a characteristic single spine pointing forward just at the beginning of the dorsal which has 13 spines. Spines poisonous. NOTE: **Siganus rivulatus** (Forsk.) (JB) as M. *Qawsalla.*(JB), E. Spinefoot. 10-25cm. +. Body light coloured with scattered small blotches and irregular, longitudinal, golden bands on the sides was listed by JB. This species has entered the Mediterranean from the Red Sea, and is apparently spreading to this area.

Fam. Gempylidae

Body long, more than X4 its height, pointed head; 1st dorsal long, 2nd dorsal and anal short terminating with free finlets; caudal forked; lower jaw longer than upper snout, conspicuous teeth.

198. **Ruvettus pretiosus** Cocco Ruvettus pretiosus (GR, GB, GD-220, GL-144, JB). M. *Ruvett.*Ruvett (JB). E. Oarfish. 1-2m. Brownish black, with bluish purple reflections. Rare, deep water. Pl.29.

Fam Trichiuridae

Very long body and laterally compressed, lower jaw longer than upper snout, teeth prominent; dorsal very long, from back of head to tail, with or without a central interruption; anal shallow, relatively short; pelvics rudiemntary, hardly present. Dorsal fin height less than half body height: 199; dorsal nearly as high as body height: 200.

199. **Lepidopus caudatus** (Euph.) Lepidopus caudatus (GB, GD-217, GL-216, JB). M. *Xabla*. Pixxixabla (GB, GD-217, GL-216); Xabla, Pixxifjamma, Pixxibandiera (GL-216). Silver scabbard fish 0.50-1.50m.+. Body silvery, paler below; fins with dark edges and initials. Occasionally frequent. Pl.29.

200. **Trichiurus lepturus** Linn. M. *Xabla denbha rqiq*. E. Large eyed hairtail. 1.60-1.00m.+. Body silvery white, fins edged dark.. Occasionally seen in groups. Pl.29.

Fam. Scombridae

Body elongated, oval in section, tapering to a point at the mouth and close to the tail; scales hardly present on hinder body; dorsal fins 2, both generally pointed and anteriorly high; 2nd dorsal and anal followed by finlets; caudal moon shaped, keels present on tail sides. Interval between 1st and 2nd dorsals X2 length of 1st dorsal base: 201; no interval between dorsals, 1st dorsal originates after pectoral base: 202; no interval between dorsals, 1st dorsal starts after pectoral base: 203; no interval between dorsals, 1st dorsal originates before pectoral base: 204; no interval between dorsals, 1st dorsal originates about pectoral base: 205; 1st and 2nd dorsals separated by interval equal to 1st dorsal base, anal originates behind origin of 2nd dorsal: 206; 1st and 2nd dorsals separated by interval one and a half times 1st dorsal base, anal originates in line with origin of 2nd dorsal: 207; no interval between dorsals, pectorals very long, reaching the 1st two finlets: 208; no interval between dorsals, pectorals short, reaching half way to base of 1st dorsal.

201. **Auxis rochei** (Riss.) Scomber bisus (GT); Auxis bison (GR, GAVG-126); Thynnus brevipinnis (GR, GAVG-129, GB); Auxis rochei (GB); Auxis bisus (GD-227); Auxis thazard (JB, GL-152). M. *Tumbrell*. Pizzintun (GT); Tumbreall (GR, GAVG-129, GB, GD-227, GL-152, JB); Sgamirru (GR, GAVG-126); Żġamirru (GB, GL-152); Mazzita (GB, GL-152); Tombitombi (GB, GL-152); Biżu (GL-152). E. Bullet tuna. 25-40cm.+. Body silvery with bluish back and dark, vertical blotches on back in a series after 1st dorsal. Frequent. Pl.29.

202. **Euthynnus alletteratus** (Raf.) Scomber allitteratus (GT); Thynnus allitteratus (GR, GAVG-128, GB); Thynnus thunnina (GB, GD-225); Euthynnus alletteratus (JB, GL-150); Euthynnus quadripunctatus (VJ). M. *Kubrita*. Kubrit (GT, GR, GAVG-128, GB); Kubrita (GD-225, GL-150, JB, VJ); Tonina (GL-150). E. Little tunny. 50-75cm.+. Back dark blue to silvery white sides and lighter underside; back irregularly mottled dark or light grey. Frequent. Pl.29.

203. **Katsuwonus pelamis** (Linn.) Gymnosarda pelamys (GL-149); Euthynnus pelamis (JB, VJ). M. *Palamit*. Palamit, Plamtu, Plamtu imperjali (GL-149); Pelamit (JB, VJ). E. Skipjack tuna. 60-80cm.+. Back bluish dark grey down to silvery underside with several longitudinal, dark, broad streaks on the hind lower sides slightly curved upwards and backwards. Formerly confused with Sarda sarda (Bloch) Frequent. Pl.29.

204. **Orcynopsis unicolor** (Geogg.S.H.) M. *Plamtu bla rigi*. E. Plain bonito. 60-80cm.+. Dark bluish grey back down to silvery white below; 1st dorsal black, but with a short posterior portion light coloured. Frequent. Formerly confused with Sarda sarda (Bloch). Pl. 29.

205. **Sarda sarda** (Bloch) Pelamys sarda (GT, GR, GAVG-131, GB, GD-226)Sarda sarda (JB, GL). M. *Plamtu*. Plamtu (GT, GB, GD-226, GL-151, JB); Palamit (GR, GAVG-131, GB, GL-151); Pelamit (GB). E. Atlantic bonito. 45-60cm.+. Dark bluish grey down to silvery and white underside; back marked with darker, longitudinal streaks, slanting down forward or curved. Frequent. Pl.30.

206. **Scomber japonicus** Hout. Scomber colias (GT, GR, GAVG-125, GD-222, GL-146); Scomber pneumatophorus (GR, GAVG-124, GB); Scomber macrophthalmus (GB); Scomber japonicus colias (JB). M. *Kavall għajnejħ kbar*. Pizzintun (young) (GT, GR, GAVG-125, GD-222, GL-146); Kavall (GR, GB, GD-222, GL-146); Okki grossu (GL-146). E. Chub mackerel. 25-35cm.+. Back bluish greenish grey with short, oblique, dark lines down to silvery and white underside; the latter may be marked irregularly greyish. Frequent. Pl.30.

207. **Scomber scombrus** Linn. Scomber scombrus (GT, GR, GAVG-123, GB, JB); Scomber scomber (GD-221, GL-145). M. *Kavall*. Kavall GT, GR, GAVG-123, GL-145); Pizzintun (GB, GD-221, GL-145, JB); Żigromblu (GL-145). E. Atlantic mackerel. 30-40cm.+. Back bluish black with undulating, oblique, black, transversal lines. Not as frequent as preceding species. Pl.30.

208. **Thunnus alalunga** (Bonn.) Scomber alalunga (GT); Thunnus alalunga (GR, GAVG-130, GB, GD-224, GL-148, JB). M. *Alonga*. Alalonga

(GT); Alonga (GR, GAVG-130, GB, GD-224, GL-148, JB); Tonn sekond (GL-148). E. Albacore. 0.90-1.00m.+. Back dark blue grey, down to silvery white underside; single fins yellowish. Often confused with some of its congeners. Frequent. Pl.30.

209. **Thunnus thynnus** (Linn.) Scomber thynnus (GT); Thynnus mediterraneus (GR, GAVG-127); Thynnus vulgaris (GB); Thynnus thynnus (GD-227); Thunnus thynnus (JB, GL-147). M. *Tonn*. Tonn (GT, GR, GAVG-127, GB, GD-223, GL-147, GB); Tunnaġġ (young) (GB, GD-223, GL-147); Tonnu (GL-147). E. Atlantic bluefin tuna. 1.50-2.50m.+. Back dark blue down to silvery and white underside; 2nd dorsal brown, other yellowish or bluish. Formerly a primary fishery with the tunnara system, said to have been introduced in Malta in 1563, caught in large numbers with related species, sometimes also some white shark and swordfish getting caught in the nets, but now has greatly declined and the tunnara fishery discontinued. Specimens caught are becoming progressively smaller. Pl.30.

Fam. Luvaridae

Anterior outline anteriorly blunt, forehead elevated, eye in line with mouth, caudal curved with long lobes; tail with one keel on each side; dorsal and anal single, shallow, both on the hinder half of body; pelvics rudimentary.

210. **Luvarus imperialis** Raf. Luvarus imperialis (GR, GB, GD-241, GL-153). M. *Tonna bajda*. Tonna bajda (GR, GD-241, GL-153); Luvaru, Pixxi serduk (GL-153). E. Luvar. 0.60-1.50m.+. Back blue down to reddish sides and silvery underside with an overall pinkish tinge on fins and body. Rare, occasional. Pl.30.

Fam. Istiophoridae

Upper snout extending out of the head into a long, swordlike snout; 2 dorsals, 1st long, reaching the 2nd dorsal which is above the 2nd anal; pelvics threadlike, elongated. Two keels on each side of tail.

211. **Tetrapterus belone** Raf. Tetrapterus belone (GR, GAVG-24, GD-219, GL-155, JB). M. *Pixxispad qasir*. Imsella imperjali (GR, GAVG-24, GD-219); Pixxispad (GL-155); Pastardella (JB). E. Mediterranean spearfish. 1.40-2.00m.+. Blackish blue back down to silvery and white underside. Pl.31.

NOTE: Often assumed to be a form of Xiphias gladius. Vernacular names of Pixxispad and Pixxispad qasir are frequently in use; the name Imsella imperjali belongs rather to Tylosurus acus (Lac.)(No.81). **Makaira albida**

Poey, listed by JB as M. Imsella imperjali, the White marlin is not within the area, and appers to refer to T. belone Raf.

Fam. Xiphiidae

Upper snout extending out of the head to form a long, swordlike snout. Only one keel on each side of tail. 2 dorsals, the first high anteriorly, down to a long, extremely shallow extention towards the 2nd dorsal.

212. **Xiphias gladius** Linn. Xiphias gladius (GT, GR, GAVG-132, GB, GD-218, GL-154, JB). M. *Pixxispad.* Pixxispad (GT, GR, GAVG-132, GB, GD-218, GL-154, JB); Spada (GL-154). E. Swordfish. 2-3m.+. Back brownish blue-black, lighter sides to paler underside. Frequent. Unfortunately, very small specimens are caught indiscriminately for the market. Pl.31.

Fam. Gobiidae

Small fishes, body elongated and slippery, eyes close to the top of the head; 2 dorsals, the 1st short, the 2nd long; pelvics below pectorals and formed into a sucker unit; 1st dorsal 6 rays (Aphia usually 4 to 7, G. Niger 5 to 7, Pomatoschistus 6 to 7); 2nd dorsal with 8 to 15 soft rays preceded by a spine; anal with 1 spiny and with from 11 to 15 soft rays (except Deltentosteus, 8 or 9); pectorals with 10-23 rays. Pelvics originate well before pectorals: 213; pelvics originate slightly after pectoral origin, 2nd dorsal 8-9rays preceded by 1 spine, anal 8-9 rays: 214; pelvics originate just in line with pectoral origin: 215; pelvics originate in line with pectoral origin, head profile elongated forward, 2nd dorsal X2 length of 1sd dorsal: 216; pelvics originate slightly ahead of pectorals, head profile anteriorly blunt, 2nd dorsal X2 length of 1st dorsal: 217; pelvics originate in line with pectoral origin, 2nd dorsal X1 2/3 length of 1st dorsal: 218; pelvics originate just after pectoral origin, 2nd dorsal abour X2 length of 1st dorsal: 218

NOTE Pelvics originate ahead of pectorals, 2nd dorsal X2 length of 1st dorsal: 219; pelvics originate just ahead of pectorals, 2nd dorsal X1 2/3 length of 1st dorsal: 220; pelvics originate well ahead of pectoral origin, 2nd dorsal X1 1/2 length of 1st dorsal: 221; pelvics originate slightly ahead of pectoral origin, 2nd dorsal nearly X2 1/2 length of 1st dorsal, eyes very small: 222.

213 **Aphia minuta** Riss. Aphia vera (GT);Aphia meridionalis (GR, GAVG-146); Aphya pellucida (GD-255, GL-235); Brachyochirus pellucidus (JB). M. *Makku.* Makku (GT, GR, GAVG-146, GD-255, GL-236, JB). E. Transparent goby. 4-5cm. Body tranparent, colourless

or slightly pink, often with tiny, dark spots. Unfortunately many other small, immature members of other species are indiscriminately caught and sold under this name. Frequent. Pl.31.

214. **Deltentosteus quadrimaculatus** (Val.) M. *Mazzun b' erba' tikek*. E. Four spotted goby. 5-8cm. Ochre grey body with irrecgular dark markings and a black spot on the end of the 1st dorsal, with 4, indistinct, pale, vertical bands on each side, ending in faint but characteristic blotches on the sides. Frequent. Pl.31.

215. **Gobius auratus** Riss. Gobius auratus (GD-252, GL-140) E. Golden goby. 10cm. Yellowish or brownish yellow with darker mottlings and two dark cheek spots. Very rare, and need confirmation. Pl.31.

216. **Gobius bucchichi** Stein. M. *Mazzun kannella*. E. Bucchich's goby. 8-10cm. Variable; ochre grey back and lighter underside with several longitudinal rows of variously sized dark blotches along the sides, and a sopot on base of pectorals. Frequent. Pl.31.

217. **Gobius cobitis** Pall. Gobius guttatus (GR, GAVG-144); Gobius exanthematicus (GD-250.GL-243); Gobius cobitis (JB). M. *Mazzun kbir*. Mazzun (GR, GAVG-144, GD-250, GL-243); Żbirr (JB, GL-243); Seracin (GL-243). E. Giant goby. 15-20cm. +. Ochre green of variable intensity with irregularly aligned scattered spots and markings on the sides; single fins may be edged white. Frequent. Pl.31.

218. **Gobius cruentatus** Gmel. Gobius cruentatus (GT, GR, GAVG-140, GD-251, GL-241). M. *Mazzun tad-demm*. Mazzun tad-demm (GT, GR, GD-251, GL-241); Mazzun (GAVG-140); Mazzun aħmar (GL-241). E. Red-mouthed goby. 10-15cm. +. Ochre background, with irregular, small, dark brown or reddish brown markings and bigger blotches along each side; mouth and face with bright red mottlings and streaks. Frequent. Pl.31.

NOTE: **Gobius geniporus** Val. Gobius geniporus (JLC). M. *Mazzun irqiq*. E. Slender goby. 14-16cm. Greenish, brownish, with an interrupted row of dark markings along each side. Shallow bottoms. An addition by JLC.

219. **Gobius niger** Linn. Gobius niger (GT, GR, GAVG-141, GD-248, GL-246, JB); Gobius jozo (GT, GR, GAVG-143, GD-253, GL-239); Goboius bicolor (GR, GAVG-142, GL-245). M. *Mazzun iswed*. Mazzun (GT, GR, GAVG-141, 142, 145, GD-248, 253, GL-239, 245, 246); Mazzun tal-ħagra (GT); Mazzun tar-ramel (GL-239); Mazzun iswed (JB). E. Black goby. 10-15cm. Variable. Ochrish brown with irregular markings and a series of dark blotches on each side and dorsal fins; males much darker. Frequent. Confused with Gobius paganellus L. Pl.31

220. **Gobius paganellus** Linn. Gobius paganellus (GT, GR, GAVG-143, GD-247, GL-244, JB); Gobius bicolor (GD-249, GL-245). M. *Mazzun tal-port.* Mazzun zbirr (GT); Mazzun (GR, GAVG-143, GD-248, 249); Żbirr (GD-247, GL-244); Mazzun tal-port (GL-244). E. Rock goby. 10-12cm. Ochrish light brown with narrow, pale, vertical bands and darker, irregular, small markings and a row of bigger, dark patches on sides; 1st dorsal often marked blue, is edged whitish. Frequent. Confused with Gobius niger L. Pl.32.

221. **Pomatoschistus minutus** (Pall.) Gobius minutus (GD-254, GL-237); M. *Mazzun tar-ramel.* Mazzun tar-ramel (GD-254, GL-237). E. Sand goby. 7-9cm. Light ochre or greyish with a black spot on 1st dorsal edged white and with irregular markings along sides, more developed vertically in males. Frequent. Pl.32.

222. **Zosterisessor ophiocephalus** (Pall.) M. *Mazzun għajnejħ żgħar.* E. Grass goby. 15-20cm.+. Ochre green with a black spot at tailbase, and dark, irregular mottlings and markings on sides and fins. Occasionally frequent. Pl.32.

Fam Callionymidae

Small fishes, body scaleless and slender; fins colourful, conspicuous and large in relation to body; eyes large, close to top of head, snout and lips elongated; 1st dorsal from 6 to 7 spines, 2nd dorsal 8 to 10. 1st dorsal 4 spines, 2nd dorsal 8-10 with no blotches: 223; 1st dorsal with 4 spines, 2nd dorsal 8-10 with blotches: 224; 1st dorsal with 4 spines, 2nd 6-7: 225; 1st dorsal with 3 spines, 2nd dorsal 7-8: 226.

223. **Callionymus lyra** Linn. Callionymus lyra (GD-256, GL-235, JB). M. *Wiżgħha ta' l-ikħal.* Wiżgħha tal-baħar (GD-256); Dragunett (JB). E. Dragonet. 15-29cm.+. Ochre light brown with blue streaks and markings all over the body and fins, with some small, black spots; females more olive coloured, and smaller than males. Not frequent. Pl.32 a(female), b(male).

224. **Callionymus maculatus** Raf.-Schm. Callionymus maculatus (GD-257, GL-234, JB). M. *Wiżgħha tat-tikek.* Wiżgħha tal-baħar (GD-257, GL-234, JB). E. Spotted dragonet. 10-15cm. Ochre pale greenish brown with various light and dark spots; head slightly purplish spotted white; 2nd dorsal with 2 rows of spots in females and 4 rows in males. Occasionally met with. Pl.32 a(female), b(male).

225. **Callionymus pusillus** Del. Callionymus dracunculus (GR); Callionymus admirabilis (GAVG-139); Callionymus festivus (GD-258, GL-233); Callionymus partenopeus (GD-259, GL-232). M. *Wiżgħha*

ta' l-ikħal żgħira. Wiżgħha tal-baħar (GR, GAVG-139). E. Small dragonet. 9-13cm. Ochrish light brown with blue streaks and markings especially on 2nd dorsal of males, and some vertical, silvery bands or markings edged dark. Occasional. Pl.32 a(female), b(male).

226. **Callionymus risso** Le Sueur. Callionymus belenus (GD-260, GL-231). M. *Wiżgħha tat-tikek suwed*. E. Blackspotted dragonet. 4-6cm.+. Ochre body with irregular markings and blackish spotting, also on 2nd dorsal of males; 1st dorsal balck in females, light in males. Frequent. Pl.33 a(female), b(male).

Fam. Blenniidae

Body scaleless, small, 1 long dorsal, 1 long anal, eyes close to top of head, profile of forehead nearly vertical; anal with 2 spines preceding rays; pelvics with 1 spine before 3 rays (4 rays in Aidablennius). Anterior height of dorsal about X3 that of anal, dorsal 12 spines and 16 rays, pectorals 14, anal 18 rays: 227; anterior height of dorsal X4 that of anal, dorsal 11 spines and 14-15 rays, anal 16 rays, pectorals 12: 228; dorsal height uniform, about X2 of anal, male with crest on head, dorsal 12 spines and 22 rays, anal 23-24 rays, pectorals 14: 229; dorsal height about X1 1/2 that of anal, dorsal 12 spines and 16-17 rays, anal 18 rays, pectorals 13: 230; tentacles over eyes X2 eye diameter, dorsal 13 spines and 18-19 rays, anal 20 rays, pectorals 14: 231; tentacles above eyes X2 eye diameter, dorsal 12 spines and 17 rays, anal 2 spines and 19rays, pectorals 14: 231

NOTE: tentacles over eye nearly equal to eye diameter, dorsal 12 spines and 21 rays, anal 21 rays, pectorals 13: 232; tentacles over eye X4 eye diameter, dorsal 12 spines and 20-21 rays, anal 22-23 rays, pectorals 14: 233.

227. **Aidablennius sphynx** Val. Blennius sphynx (GL-229). M. *Budakkra lewn iż-żebbuġ*. E. Sphynx blenny. 5-8cm. olive background, with some brownish, green, broad, irregular, vertical or oblique lines margined white or black on sides, continuous with the dorsal fin at the top; a red blotch, edged dark behind the eye. Frequent.

228. **Blennius ocellaris** Linn. Blennius ocellaris (GT, GR, GAVG-148, GD-261, GL-230, JB). M. *Budakkra ta' l-għajn*. Budakkra ta' l-għajn (GT, GR, GAVG-148, GD-261, GL-230). E. Butterfly blenny. 10-15cm.+. Variable, mainly greenish or fawn with some darker, irregular, broad, vertical bands on the sides, the posterior ones continuous with the dorsal fin; a big, black, round blotch edged white on the dorsal fin. Frequent. Pl.33.

229. **Lipophrys pavo** (Riss.) Ichthyocorus pavo (GR, GAVG-149); Blennius pavo (GD-262, GL-228, JB). M. *Budakkra ta' l-għalla*. E. Crested blenny. 8-10cm.+. Olive or yellowish green or ochre with blue, vertical, wavy lines associated with darker bands and preceded by spots; a blue or black, round blotch margined lilac behind the eye; an orange or yellow crest develops on the head of males in the mating season. Frequent. Pl.33 (male).

230. **Lipophrys trigloides** (Val.) Blennius pholis (GT, GD-265, GL-224); Blennius laevis (GR, GAVG-150). M. *Bużullieqa*. Bużullieqa (GT, GR, GAVG-150, GD-265, GL-224). E. Small shanny. 10-13cm. Variable; ochre, greenish, greyish yellowish, variously marked with indistinct, vertical bars; males become dark brown during mating season. Frequent. Pl.33.

NOTE: **Lipophrys pholis** (Linn.) E. Shanny, has for long been recorded (GT, GR, GAVG-150, GD-265, GL-224), but apparently must have been a mistaken identification of Lipophrys trigloides Val. which is very similar to it morphologically, in colour and habits, but does not attain its length. L. trigloides has a groove between the eyes and less of soft rays. **Blennius basilicus** (Val.), E. Zebra shanny. Dorsal uniformly high, about X2 anal height, males with head crest, dorsal 12 spines and 24-25 rays, anal two spines and 25-26 rays, pectorals 14, has been recorded as common in Malta (GJ-p.45), but its distribution appears to be further north, and perhaps may be attributed to L.pavo (Riss.), which is quite similar.

231.**Parablennius gattorugine** (Brunn.) Blennius galerita (GT); Blennius gattorugine (GR, GAVG-147, GD-264, GL-225, JB). M. *Budakkra tal-qawwi*. Budakkra (GT, GR, GAVG-147, GD-264, GL-225); Budakkra tal-qawwi (JB). E. Tompot blenny. 20-25cm.+. Brownish ochre or reddish brown with some darker, broad, wavy, vertical bands on the sides. Frequent. Pl.33.

NOTE: **Parablennius incognitus** (Bath) Parablennius incognitus (JLC). 5-6cm. Brownish, greyish, greenish with darker, vertical bands on sides; males become colourful, including red, during mating season. Recorded (JLC) in shallow water. **Parablennius svonimiri** (Kol.) Blennius svonimiri (GJ). E. Svonimir's blenny, 6-7cm. Dorsal 12 spines and 18 rays, anal 2 spines and 19-20rays, pectorals 14; brown, with a row of white spots along back below dorsal, and scattered, small dark spots over the body and head. Said to be frequent in Malta, (GJ).

232. **Parablennius sanguinoletus** (Pall.) Blennius sanguinoletus (GL-227, JB). M. *Budakkra ħamra*. Budakkra ħamra (JB). E. Red speckled

blenny. 13-16cm. +. Variable, greyish or ochrish green with darker markings, spots and streaks, which may be red or rosy. Occasionally frequent. Pl.33.

233. **Parablennius tentacularis** (Brunn.) Blennius tentacularis (GT, GD-263, GL-226). M. *Budakkra kannella*. Pixxi gatt (GT). E. Horned blenny. 10-15cm. Brownish body with numerous dark spots, and most often some broad, irregular, vertical or slightly transversal bands on the sides; a large, dark spot on the first few dorsal spines. Frequent. Pl.33.

NOTE: **Scartella cristata** (Linn.) Scartella cristata (JLC). Tentacles over eyes shorter than eye diameter and more numerous over the head; dorsal 12 spines and 14-15 rays, anal 2 spines and 16 rays, pectorals 14. Brownish, greenish, with indistinct, darker, vertical bands on sides and some white spots towards edges and bases of fins. Recorded in shallow water (JLC).

Fam. Clinidae

Similar to Blenniidae. Body more slender but with microscopic scales, head not so robust.

234. **Clinitrachus argentatus** (Riss.) Clinus variabilis (GR); Clinus argentatus (GAVG-152); Cristiceps argentatus (GD-266, GL-222). M. *Budakkra tal-fidda*. E. Silver clinid. 8-10cm. Olive ochre with silvery blotches, forming irregular, broad, vertical bands, included in the dorsal, alternating with reddish brown. Frequent. Pl.34.

Fam. Tripteriigidae

1 dorsal, but appears as 3, the 1st very small, the second with anterior spines equal to body height, the 3rd with only soft rays; eye large.

235. **Tripterygion tripteronotus** (Riss.) Tripterygion nasus (GR, GAVG-151, GD-267, GL-223); Tripterygion tripteronotus (JB). M. *Budakkra rasha sewda*. Budakkra (GL-223); Budakkra bżarija (JB). E. Blackheaded three-finned blenny. 5-7cm. +. Overall grey-greenish with darker head, and dark, wide, vertical bands on sides; males have a black head and a reddish body. Frequent. Pl.34(male).

Fam. Ophidiidae

Body elongated with eyes close to the snout; pelvics look like barbels on the lower jaw; dorsal and anal continuous with caudal. Barbel-like pelvics about X2 eye diameter: 236; barbel-like pelvics X4 or X4 eye diameter: 237.

236. **Ophidion barbatum** Linn. Ophidion barbatum (GT, GR, GAVG-51, GD-75, GL-247, JB, VJ). M. *Ballottra tal-ħama*. Ballottra tar-ramel GT, GR, GAVG-51, GD-75); Ballottra tal-baħar (GL-247); Ballottra (JB); Ballottra tal-ħama (VJ). E. Bearded ophidion. 15-20cm. +. Ochre brownish or reddish brown with median fins edged black; underside silvery. Frequent. Pl.34.

NOTE: **Ophidion rochei** Mull., is extremely similar to O. barbatum L., but is slightly darker and longer; further investigation may prove that it may also be present with the above, as its distribution is closer to central Mediterranean, and is easily mistaken for it.

237. **Parophidion vassalli** Riss. Ophidion vassalli (GD-76, GL-248); Parophidion vassalli (VJ). M. *Ballottra ħamranija*. Ballottra GD, GL-248); Ballottra ħamranija (VJ). E. Cuskeel. 18-22cm. +. Fawn-ochre or flesh-coloured with red fins, underside white. Rare. Pl.34.

Fam. Carapidae

Body very delicate, smooth and narrowing thinly to a tapering tail; dorsal very long and shallow, continuous with the caudal and the higher, long anal.

238. **Carapus acus** (Brunn.) Fierasfer acus (GIOG-2, GD-77, GL-249). M. *Ħuta tal-ħjar*. E. Pearlfish. 15-20cm. Transparent body with some yellowish or silvery golden markings, often with reddish spots. Frequent inside hinder alimentary tract of sea cucumbers (M. *Ħjar tal-baħar*). Pl.34.

Fam. Centrolophidae

Body robust, snout blunt, eyes very close to mouth. 1 long dorsal with spines and rays, the anal being about 1/2 its length. Snout outline angular: 239; snout outline rounded: 240.

239. **Centrolophus niger** (Gmel.) Centrolophus pompylus GB, GD-244, GL-250); Centrolophus niger (JB). M. *Lampuka tat-torok*. Lampuka tat-torok (GB, GD-244, GL-250); Fanfru barrani (GB). E. Blackfish. 0.80-1.20m. +. Uniform dark reddish brown or bluish brown sometimes slightly marked; underside paler; vertical, lateral bars may be present in small specimens. Rare. Pl.34.

240. **Schedophilus ovalis** (Val.) Schedophilus medusophagus (GL-251). *Ħuta tal-bram*. E. Imperial blackfish. 50-70cm. +. Olive green, yellowish green, marbled darker with the same colours; abdomen paler. Occasionally met with among floating rubbish, jellyfish and surface plankton. Pl.34.

NOTE: Schedophilus medusophagus Cocco, a similar species formerly recorded (GL-251), should be referred to S. ovalis Val.

Fam. Stromateidae

Body laterally compressed, 1 dorsal, 1 anal, both elongated, high anteriorly, and lower towards the deeply forked tail; body very oval, its length about X2 height.

241. **Stromateus fiatola** Linn. Stromateus fiatola (GD-245, GL-252, JB). M. *Strilja bagħlija*. Bagħal ta' l-istillerija (GD-245); Lampuka ta' l-istillerija (GL-252); Strilja bagħlija (JB, GL-252). E. Butterfish. 30-40cm. +. Bluish green with oval, golden blotches or spots on sides which may have indistinct, vertical, dark or hazy bands in the smaller specimens; abdomen silvery. Not common. Pl.35.

Fam. Sphyraenidae

Body elongated, shallow, laterally compressed, smooth, long, pointed, lower jaw longer than upper snout; 2 distinct dorsal, 2nd opposed to anal, 1st with 5 spines opposed to pelvics.

242. **Sphyraena sphyraena** (Linn.) Esox sphyraena (GT); Sphyraena spet (GR, GAVG-23, GD-130, GL-261); Sphyraena sphyraena (JB). M. *Liżż*. Liżż (GT, GR, GAVG-23, GD-130, GL-261, JB); Alluzz, Luzzu (GL-261). E. Barracuda. 40-70cm. +. Dark, greenish olive back down to silvery abdomen with or without a yellow, longitudinal band alongside. Frequent. Pl.34.

NOTE: **Sphyraena chrysotaenia** Klunz. Sphyraena obtusata (JB). E. Bluntjaw barracuda (/Obtuse barracuda). M. *Liżż ta' lvant*. Liżż tal-vant (JB), with large eyes and higher body profile, listed by JB, appears to be entering through the Suez Canal, and may be occasionally met with in Central Mediterranean.

Fam. Mugilidae

Elongated, robust body, not very compressed laterally, with head dorso-ventrally compressed, pointed at the snout; eyes close to the front of the head and the small mouth; 2 distinct dorsals, 1st with 4 spines, 2nd with 1 spine preceding 8 rays; lateral line not evident. Upper lip relatively thick:243; forehead scales do not reach beyond anterior eye level: 244; forehead scales reach beyond anterior eye level: 245, 246; pupil normally obscured by fatty tissue around it: 247; upper lip rather thick: 248.

243. **Chelon labrosus** (Riss.) Mugil chelo (GR, GAVG-110, GD-127, GL-258, JB). M. *Mulett kaplat*. Mulett (GR, GAVG-110, GD-127, GL-258); Kaplat (JB, GL-258). E. Thicklipped grey mullet. 30-50 cm.+. Dark, bluish grey back, silvery sides and abdomen, with yellowish, darker, often indistinct, longitudinal band on sides. Frequent. Pl.35.

244. **Liza aurata** (Riss.) Mugil auratus (GR, GAVG-113, GD-124, GL-256, JB, VJ). M. *Mulett taċ-ċarruta safra*. Mulett taċ-ċarruta safra (GR, GAVG-113, GD-124, GL-256); Mulett ta' l-imċarrta, Mulett, Lostru (GL-256); Mulett tal-misluta (JB, VJ). E. Golden grey maullet. 30-40cm.+. Dark grey back to silvery on flanks and abdomen; operculum marked golden yellow. Not common. Pl.35.

245. **Liza ramada** (Riss.) Mugil capito (GR, GAVG-112, GD-123, GL-255, JB). M. *Mulett ta' l-imċarrat*. Mulett ta' l-imċarrat (GR, GAVG-112, GD-123, GL-255); Mulett (GL-255). E. Thinlipped grey mullet. 30-40cm.+. Brownish grey back with bluish, metallic reflections, abdomen silvery; Longitudinal lines along sides are weakly marked; pectorals based with a black spot. Frequent. Pl.35.

246. **Liza saliens** (Riss.) Mugil saliens (GR, GAVG-114, GD-125, GL-257, JB). M. *Mulett buri*. Buri (singular) (GR, GAVG-114, GL-257); Bwir (plural) (GR, GAVG-114, GD-125, GL-257); Mulett buri (JB); Mulett (GL-257). E. Leaping mullet. 20-30cm.+. Back dark grey down to silvery abdomen; flanks with a few, longitudinal, dark lines. Common. Pl.35.

247. **Mugil cephalus** Linn. Mugil cephalus (GT, GR, GAVG-109, GD-122, GL-253, JB, VJ). M. *Mulett ta' l-iswed*. Mulett (GT, GL-253); Kaplat (GT, GR, GAVG-109, GD-122, GL-253); Mulett ta' l-iswed (JB, VJ). E. Flatheaded grey mullet. 50-80cm.+. Dark greenish or bluish grey, abdomen silvery, flanks with longitudinal, dark grey lines. Common. Pl.35.

248. **Oedalechilus labeo** (Cuv.) Mugil labeo (GR, GAVG-111, GD-126, GL-254, JB). M. *Mulett bobin*. Bobin (GR, GAVG-111, GD-126, GL-254); Mulett (GL-254); Kaplat buri (JB). E. Boxlip mullet. 15-20cm.+. Dark or bluish grey, abdomen silvery grey; flanks with golden grey longitudinal lines. Common. Pl.35.

Fam. Atherinidae

Elongated body, with head region more robust than rest of body; 2 spaced dorsals, 2nd opposed and about equal in length and height to anal. Space interval between dorsals less than base length of 1st dorsal: 249; space interval between dorsals more than base length of 1st dorsal: 250.

249. **Atherina hepsetus** Linn. Atherina hepsetus (GT, GR, GAVG-107, GD-129, GL-260, JB). M. *Kurunella.* Kurunella GT, GR, GAVG-107, GD-129, GL-260, JB); Kurunetta (GL:-260). E. Sand smelt. 15-20cm. +. Back bluish or greenish grey regularly spotted black; flanks without spots, but with a longitudinal, silvery stripe. Frequent. Pl.36.

250. **Atherina boyeri** Riss. Atherina boyeri (GR, GAVG-108, GD-128, GL-259, JB); Atherina mochon (JB). M. *Kurunella għajnejh kbar.* Kurunella (GR, GAVG-108, GD-128, GL-259, JB); Kurunetta (GL-259). E. Boyer's sand smelt. 8-10cm. +. Back bluish or greenish grey with blackish spots, with a silvery line on the side accompanied by 1 or 2 longitudinal rows of black spots; abdomen white. Frequent. Pl.36.

Fam. Scorpaenidae

Body thick, with spiny, massive head region; eyes at forehead outline; 1 dorsal with spines preceding rays; anal with 3 spines preceding rays. No soft projections on head region, mouth dark inside: 251; soft projections above eyes, anal origin in line with dorsal soft rays origin: 252; soft projections above eyes, scales small, anal originated ahead of dorsal soft rays: 253; soft projections above eyes, anal originates slightly behind origin of dorsal soft rays: 254. Emerge mostly by night, when body often exhibits 2 or 3 transverse red or brownish bands. They also emit croaking sounds at night.

251 **Helicolenus dactylopterus** (Del.) Sebastes imperialis (GR, GAVG); Sebastes dactylopterus (GD-194, GL-265); Helicolenus dactylopterus (JB, VJ). M. *Ċippullażża ta' l-għajn.* Ċippullażża ta' għajnha (GR); Ċippullażża tal-fond (GD-194); Ċippullażża ta' l-għajn (GD-194, GL-265); Skorfna imperjali (GL-265, JB). E. Rockfish. 20-30cm. +. Body red, with or without vertical brown bands; underside paler; there is a dark spot in the middle of the dorsal. The Mediterranean species belongs to the subspecies dactylopterus. Frequent. Pl.36.

252. **Scorpaena notata** Raf. Scorpaena ustulata (GD-193, GL-264); Scorpaena notata (JB, VJ). M. *Skorfna tat-tebgħa.* Skorfna (GD-193); Skorfnott (JB); Skorfna tat-tebgħa (VJ). E. Small scorpionfish. 12-15cm. +. Greyish or brownish red or rosy, all slightly marked blackish, with an oblong, large, black blotch on spiny dorsal. Frequent. Pl.36.

253. **Scorpaena porcus** Linn. Scorpaena porcus (GT, GR, GAVG-82, GD-191, GL-262, JB). M. *Skorfna sewda.* Slorfna (GT, GR,

GAVG-82, GD-191, GL-262); Skorfna sewda (JB). E. Black scorpionfish. 14-20cm.+. Greyish brown freckled darker and marked darker all over; caudal banded vertically and a pale patch on dorsal often grey; abdomen rosy grey. Common. Pl.36.

254. **Scorpaena scrofa** Linn. Scorpaena scrofa (GT, GR, GAVG-81, GD-192, GL-263, JB). M. *Ċippullażża*. Ċippullażża (GT, GR, GAVG-81, GD-192, GL-263, JB) Skorfna, Skorfna ħamra (GL-263). E. Red scorpionfish. 30-40cm.+. Red of varying intensity or brownish red, with scattered, brownish markings often with a black, elongated blotch on dorsal. Common. Pl.36.

NOTE: **Scorpaena maderensis** Val. Scorpaena maderensis (VJ). M. *Skorfna tal-Madejra*.(VJ). E. Madeira rockfish. 8-10cm.+. has been listed for Malta. (VJ). Its presence in the Mediterranean is sporadically recorded.

Fam. Triglidae

Body elongated, head region robust and spiny with forehead frofile falling steeply down at eye region to a level base terminating at the mouth; lower jaw shorter than the snout; pectorals with 3 spines free, serving as ground feelers; dorsals 2. Pectorals reach origin of 2nd dorsal: 255; pectorals reach to 1st 2 rays of 2nd dorsal, 1st dorsal about X2 height of 2nd dorsal, with 2 spines much longer than the rest: 256; pectorals reach 1st 2 rays of 2nd dorsal, 1st dorsal about 1 1/2 height of 2nd dorsal, but is less than 152 its length: 257; pectorals reach 1st 2 rays of 2nd dorsal, 1st dorsal about 1 1/2 height of 2nd dorsal, but more than 1/2 its length: 258; pectorals reach to 1st 4 rays of 2nd dorsal: 259, 260; pectorals reach middle of 2nd dorsal: 261.

255. **Aspitrigla cuculus** (Linn.) Trigla cuculus (GT, GR, GAVG-77, GL-267; Aspitrigla cuculus (JB). M. *Żumbrell għadma*. Żumbrell (GT, GR, GAVG-77, GL-267); Gallinetta (GR); Gallina, Għadma, Żumbrell (GL-267). E. Red gurnard. 25-30cm.+. Red back spreading to pinkish and white below; fins yellowish or pinkish, anal with pale base. Frequent. Pl.37.

256. **Aspitrigla obscura** (Linn.) Trigla cuculus (GAVG-76); Trigla obscura (GD-186, GL-269); Trigla pini (GD-187); Aspitrigla obscura (JB). M. *Żumbrell spanjulett*. Zombrell (GAVG-76, GL-269); Żumbrell (GD-116, GL-269); Kappun (GL-269); Spanjulett (JB, GL-269). E. Longfin gurnard. 20-30cm.+. Back red down to lighter abdomen through pinkish flanks; fins pinkish pectorals bluish black. Not common. Pl.37.

257. **Eutrigla gurnardus** (Linn.) Trigla gurnardus (GD-184, GL-270); Trilja milvus (GD-185, GL-271); Eutrigla gurnardus (JB). M. *Gallina griża*. Gallina (GD-185, GL-271); Trigla, Kappun tar-ramel (GL-270); Gallina griża (JB, GL-270). E. Grey gurnard. 25-35cm.+. Variable, from reddish, pinkish, greyish, greyish green, with small, white spots scattered all over; underside pale; 1st dorsal with a black spot. Frequent in some localities. Pl.37.

258. **Lepidotrigla cavillone** (Lac.) Trigla aspera (GD-189, GL-273); Lepidotrigla cavillone (JB). M. *Żumbrell aħrax*. Żumbrell (JB, GL-273); Zombrell, Spanjulett, Gallina, Kappun (GL-273). Large-scaled gurnard. 15-20cm. Body red or greyish red, abdomen whitish; pectorals usually pale at their base. Not frequent. Pl.37.

259. **Trigla lucerna** Linn. Trigla hirundo (GT); Trigla corax (GR, GAVG-78, GD-183); Trigla lucerna (JB, GL-272). M. *Gallinetta*. Gallinetta (GT, GR, GAVG-78, GD-183, JB, GL-272); Tiġieġa (GT); Bukassa, Sibulassa, Zumbrell, Zombrell, Kappun (GL-272). E. Tub gurnard. 25-40cm.+. Brownish red or reddish to rosy yellow with some indistinct, light blotches; flanks and abdomen whitish; pectorals purplish black with some light spots, edged blue or purplish. Frequent. Pl.37.

260. **Trigla lyra** Linn. Trigla lyra (GT, GR, GAVG-76, GD-182, GL-268, JB). M. *Għadma*. Għadma (GT, GR, GAVG-76, GD-182, GL-268); Gallina (GR, GL-268); Tiġieġa tal-baħar (GR); Gallinetta (JB, GL-268); Żumbrell, Kappun (GL-268). E. Piper gurnard. 25-40cm.+. Red, down to pale underside; fins edged blue or mostly spotted blue. Frequent. Pl.37.

261. **Trigloporus lastoviza** (Brunn.) Trigla lineata (GR, GD-188, GL-266); Trigla garrulus (GAVG-75); Trigloporus lastoviza (JB). M. *Gallinetta tar-rigi*. Żumbrell (GR, GD-188, GL-266); Gallinetta (GAVG-75, GL-266); Zombrell, Pixxipapa (GL-266); Gallinetta tar-rigi (JB, VJ). E. Streaked gurnard. 20-30cm.+. Red, often marked blackish, with very thin, vertical markings, abdomen whitish; fins spotted blue. Frequent. Pl.38.

Fam. Peristediidae

Body similar to that of Triglidae, but characterised by 2, long, bony projections from the side of the lower head, forming 2 prongs extending well ahead of the lower jaw.

262. **Peristedion cataphractum** Linn. Trigla cataphracta (GT); Peristedion cataphractum (GR, GAVG-79, GD-190, GL-274, JB). M.

Pixxikornutu. Pixxikornutu (GT, GR, GAVG-79, GD-190, GL-274, JB); Buqarn, Armata (GL-274). E, Armed gurnard 20-30cm. +. Red, down to paler underside. Common. Pl.38.

Fam. Dactylopteridae

Body similar to triglidae, but head more robust and rectangular, and characterised by very large, wing-like pectorals, which, when folded and closed back, extend to caudal.

263. **Dactylopterus volitans** Linn. Trigla volitans (GT); Dactylopterus volitans (GR, GAVG-80, GD-181, GL-275, JB); Cephalacanthus volitans (VJ). M. *Bies*. Bies (GT, GR, GAVG-80, GD-181, GL-275); Falkun (GT, GR, GAVG-80, GL-275); Rundinella, Rondinella, Garnaw, Ħamiema, Pixxiseqer (GL-275). E. Flying gurnard. 30-40cm. +. Reddish, brownish, greyish, marked darker red and black, underside pale; fins grey marked with blue and black blotches and spots. Does not fly out of water, but uses "wings" only for display; emits a croak when caught. Frequent. Pl.38.

Fam. Citharidae

Body laterally extremely compressed and oval, and rests on its right side on the sea bed, with eyes developing on the left side; right eye margin closely in contact with dorsal origin.

264. **Citharus linguatula** (Linn.) Eucitharus linguatula (GD-94, GL-284); Citharus linguatula (JB); Citharus macrolepidotus (VJ). M. *Lingwata tal-qxur kbar*. Lingwata (GD-94, GL-284); Ingwata ta' l-iskwami (JB); Lingwata ta' l-iskwami (VJ). E. Spotted flounder. 20-28cm. Ochrish grey, with posterior scale margin darker; close to caudal base may be 2 dark blotches; eyeless side pale. Not frequent. Pl.38.

Fam. Scophthalmidae

Body laterally extremely compressed, oval, lies on the right side on sea bed, eyes developing on the left side; right eye close to, but not in contact with dorsal origin. Left side(eyed) with bony tubercles: 265; left side (eyed) with no bony tubercles: 266.

265. **Psetta maxima** (Linn.) Rhombus maximus (GR, GAVG-59, GD-90, GL-277). M. *Barbun imperjali*. Barbun imperjali (GR, GD-90, GL-277, JB); Lingwata imperjali (GL-277). E. Turbot. 40-50cm. +. Greenish grey to yellowish ochrish brown speckled all over irregularly with olive

grey and black; very variable. The mediterranean species belongs to the subspecies maxima. Not frequent. Pl.38.

NOTE: Phrynorhombus regius (Bonn.), previously recorded (GL-280), as Phrynorhombus unimaculatus Riss., is now to be considered as having been a form of Psetta maxima (Linn.).

266. **Scophthalmus rhombus** (Linn.) Pleuronectes rhombus (GT); Rhombus laevis (GR, GAVG-58, GD-91, GL-278); Scophthalmus rhombus (JB, VJ). M. *Barbun*. (GT, GR, GAVG-58, GD-91, GL-278); Barbun lixx, Lingwata lixxa (GL-278); Patrun (JB, GL-278, VJ). E. Brill. 30-45cm. +. Yellowish grey or greenish brown or olive irregularly marked with dark brown; eyeless side white. Frequent. Pl.38.

NOTE: **Psettodes belcheri** Benn. 30cm. +. Eyes either on left or on right side, eyed side grey, eyeless side white, was obtained from Valletta market in 1971 (GL-303), but it belongs to eastern Atlantic and appears to have been imported through Italian fishermen.

Fam. Bothidae

Body laterally extremely compressed, oval, and rests on its right side on seabed, eyes developing on the left side. Eyes close together, 1st dorsal rays longer than the rest: 267; eyes close together, 1st dorsal rays shorter than the rest, dorsal originates near right eye: 268; eyes close together, 1st dorsal rays shorter than the rest, dorsal originates in line with the space between eyes: 269; eyes far from, each other: 270.

267. **Arnoglossus imperialis** (Raf.) Arnoglossus bosci (GD-93, GL-283). M.*Lingwata*. Lingwata (GL-283); Lingwata ta' l-għajnejn (GL-283, VJ), (this Maltese name is applicable to No.272). E. Four-spotted Scaldfish. 20-25cm. Ochrish brown or greyish ochre, eyeless side white; anal and dorsal with black spots, pelvics marked dark. Apparently rare.

268. **Arnoglossus kessleri** Schn. Arnoglossus grohmanni (GL-281, JB); Arnoglossus kessleri (VJ). M. *Lingwata tat-tikek suwed*. Lingwata (GL-281); Ingwata tal-faxx (JB); Lingwata tal-faxx (VJ). E. Kessler's scaldfish. 7-9cm. Brown or reddish grey with black spots or frecklings. Not frequent. Pl.39.

269. **Arnoglossus laterna** (Walb.) Arnoglossus laterna (GD-92, GL-282, JB, VJ). M. *Lingwata lixxa*. Lingwata (GL-282); Ingwata lixxa (JB); Lingwata lixxa (GL-282, VJ). E. Scaldfish. 14-18cm. +. Light brown or yellowish grey with or without irregular, brownish freckles; eyeless side white or greyish. Sometimes frequent. Pl.39.

NOTE: **Arnoglossus thori** Kyle. Arnoglossus thori (VJ). M. *Lingwata tax-xulliefa*, (VJ). is characterised by a long, membranous 2nd dorsal ray, known in the north and western Mediterranean, has been listed for Malta. (VJ).

270. **Bothus podas** (Del.) Rhomboidichthys podas (GL-279); Bothus podas (JB). M. *Barbun għajnejh imbegħda*. Barbun tal-għajn (JB). E. Wide eyed flounder. 30-40cm. +. Ochrish brown freckled with pale blotches circled brown or light blue; head marbled yellow. The Mediterranean species belongs to the subspecies podas. Not frequent. Pl.39.

Fam. Pleuronectidae

Flatfishes with dorsal originating at eye level, prominent lateral line on both sides, eyes on the right side.

NOTE: Platichthys flesus (Linn.) E. Flounder, M. Barbun (JB) and Pleuronectes platessa Linn., E. Plaice, M. Barbun tat-tbajja (JB) have both been listed for Malta (JB), but are outside our area, and have not been recorded by others.

Fam. Soleidae

Body laterally extremely compressed, resting on sea bed on its left side, eyes developing on the right side; Anal closer to caudal than is the dorsal: 271; 272 to 277 mostly distinguishable by colour pattern.

271. **Buglossidium luteum** (Riss.) Solea lutea (JB); Buglossidium luteum (VJ). M. *Lingwata safra*. Ingwata safra (JB); Lingwata safra (VJ). E. Yellow sole. 10-12cm.+. Ochre yellow with scattered brownish frecklings, and a few, greyish, irregular, vertical, narrow bands on eyed side; unpaired fins with some vertical, dark lines. Rather rare. Pl.39.

272. **Microchirus ocellatus** (Linn.) Solea ocellata (GD-97, GL-287); Solea ocellaris (JB); Microchirus ocellatus (VJ). M. *Lingwata ta' l-għajnejn*. Lingwata ta' l-għajnejn (GL-287); Ingwata ta' l-għajn (JB); Lingwata ta' l-għajn (VJ). E. Four eyed sole. 15-20cm. Greyish purplish yellow, with a large blotch on the lateral line, and 4 or 5 smaller, round spots encircled pale yellow or golden, scattered close to dorsal and anal. Frequent. Pl.39.

273. **Microchirus variegatus** (Don.) Solea variegata (GL-289); Microchirus variegatus (VJ). M. *Lingwata tar-rigi*. Lingwata tar-rigi (VJ). E. Thickback sole. 15-20cm. Brownish or yellowish grey mostly with 6 or 7 darker, irregular, transversal bands across the eyed side. Frequent. Pl.39.

274. **Microchirus hispidus** Raf. Solea monochir (GR, GAVG-61, GD-99, GL-290); Monochirus hispidus (JB, VJ). M. *Lingwata ħarxa*. Busuf (GD-99, GL-290, JB); Lingwata ħarxa, Lingwata piluża (GL-290); Lingwata xewwekija (VJ). E. Whiskered sole. 15-20cm. Pectoral fin absent from eyeless side; scales harsh. Ochre brownish, with darker, irregular patches and a weak, round spot closer to the tail. Occasionally frequent. Pl.39.

275. **Solea impar** Benn. Solea impar (GL-288). M. *Lingwata tat-tikek kohol*. Lingwata (GL-288). E. Adriatic sole. 15-20cm.+. Very variable; greenish or yellowish grey brown, with small, darker, scattered, irregular blotches, blue when fresh; fins edged white eyeless side pale. Frequent. Pl.40.

276. **Solea kleinii** (Riss.) Solea kleinii (GD-96, GL-286, JB). M. *Lingwata tat-tikek bojod*. Lingwata (GD-96); Ingwata skura (JB). E. Klein's sole. 25-35cm.+. Brownish, with a few blackish-greyish dots or blotches and many scattered white spots; eyeless side pale; unpaired fins mostly edged black; right pectoral with a black spot. Frequent. Pl.40.

277. **Solea vulgaris** Quen. Pleuronectes solea (GT); Solea vulgaris (GR, GAVG-60, GD-95, JB, VJ); Solea solea (GL-285). M. *Lingwata komuni*. Lingwata (GT, GR, GAVG-60, GD-95, GL-285); Ingwata tar-rig (JB); Lingwata tar-rig (VJ). E. Common sole. 40-50cm.+. Greyish or greenish brown, with irregular brownish or blackish markings; right pectoral tipped black, caudal edge broadly dark; eyeless side white, sometimes with some small, insignificant spots. Frequent. Pl.40.

Fam. Echeneididae

Elongated, slender body, head flattened, surmounted by 1st dorsal modified into an elongated disc with sucker laminae, by which the fish could attach itself to larger fish, boats, etc. Disc laminae more than 20:278; disc laminae not more than 20: 279.

278. **Echeneis naucrates** Linn. Echeneis naucrates (GIOG-4, GD-228, GL-292, VJ). M. *Remora tal-faxx*. Pixxi tmun (GD-228); Remora tal-faxx iswed (VJ). E. Remora (/Sharksucker). 30-50cm.+. Greyish or dark brown with or without a longitudinal band on the side, or rarely black margined white. Rare. Pl.40.

279. **Remora remora** (Linn.) Echeneis remora (GR, GAVG-57, GD-229, GL-291); Remora remora (JB, VJ). M. *Remora komuni*. Pixxitmun (GR, GAVG-57, GD-229, GL-291); Remora (JB, GL-291); Remora komuni (VJ); Buwaħħal (GL-291). E. Common remora. 20-30cm.+.

Brownish, purplish brown or greenish blue, underside pale. Frequent. Pl.40.

Fam. Balistidae

Body laterally compressed, high, oval, mouth small, eye small, close to 1st dorsal; 2nd dorsal and anal are similar and opposed; operculum a simple, small slit.

280. **Balistes carolinensis** Gmel. Balistes capriscus (GIOG-5, GD-62, GL-293); Balistes carolinensis (JB). M. *Ħmar*. Ħmar (GIOG-5, GD-62, GL-293, JB). E. Grey triggerfish. 30-40cm.+. Variable; mainly greenish or purplish brown or yellowish greyish brown, irregularly marked, streaked and spotted blue, the latter colour soon disappearing after death. Frequent. Pl.40.

NOTE: Small specimens, without the blue colouration, with elongated blotches on the sides, 1st dorsal with one effective spine, and no caudal extensions, occasionaly taken, are assumed to be the young of B. carolinensis, but these appear to be **Stephanolepis diaspros** (Fras.-Brunn). Fam. **Monacanthidae** which are immigrating into the Mediterranean through the Suez Canal, and are already known from central Mediterranean.

Fam. Tetraodontidae

Body without scales but with some spiny projections; lower body can be inflated; mouth very small, far from the small eye. Dorsal and anal single, opposed far bach in the body.

281. **Lagocephalus lagocephalus** (Linn.) Tetraodon lagocephalus (GT); Lagocephalus pennanti (GR, GAVG-156); Lagocephalus lagocephalus (GD-61, GL-273). M. *Ħmar jintefaħ*. Bużaqq (GT); Ħmar (GR, GAVG-156, GD-61, GL-273); Bagħal, Pala tal-baħar (GL-273). E. Pufferfish. 30-40cm.+. Greeninsh, bluish, greyish green; underside pale yellow or white. Puffs itself up into a spiny ball when alarmed. Occasionally met with. Pl.40 a(normal condition), b(body inflated).

Fam. Molidae

Body very rounded, oval, laterally compressed; eyes, mouth and pectorals all diminutive in relation to body; dorsal and anal single, extremely high in relation to base, opposed far back in the body. Body height X2/3 of length, mouth a small horizontal slit: 282; body X2 height, mouth a small vertical slit: 283.

282. **Mola mola** (Linn.) Diodon mola (GT); Mola aspera (GR);

Orthagoriscus mola (GAVG-155, GD-59, GL-295); Mola mola (JB). M. *Qamar*. Qamar (GT, GR, GAVG-155); Pixxiluna (GAVG-155, GL-295); Mola (GD-59, GL-295); Pixxi mola (GR); Pixxitambur (GL-295). E. Ocean sunfish. 1-2m.+. Brown back down to greyish underside with silvery reflections. Occasionally met with. Pl.41.

283. **Ranzania laevis** (Penn.) Orthagoriscus truncatus (GD-60, GL-296). M. *Qamar tawwali*. Pixxiluna, Mola, Pixxitambur (GL-296). E. Oblong sunfish. 50-70cm.+. Brown or bluish brown back, with some pale, vertical or oblique lines, down to silvery white underside. Very rare. Pl.41.

Fam. Gobiesocidae

Body and snout elongated, scaleless, 1 dorsal opposed but not equal to the anal, both close to the caudal; pelvics developed into a ventral sucker. Dorsal up to 7 rays, anal up to 8: 284; dorsal over 13 rays, anal over 9, back humped posterior to pectoral tip, anal originates slightly after dorsal origin: 285; dorsal over 13 rays, anal over 9, back humped over pectoral base and tip, anal originates far from dorsal: 286.

284. **Diplecogaster bimaculata** (Bonn.) Lepadogaster bimaculatus (GD-120, GL-299). M. *Buwaħħal rasu qasira*. Buwaħħal (GD-120, GL-299). E. Two-spotted clingfish. 3-4cm. Pale reddish or brownish, with blackish striations on the sides, with or without one large, purplish blotch, tinged white on each side. The Mediterranean species belongs to the subspecies bimaculata. Not rare. Pl.41.

285. **Lepadogaster candollei** Riss. Lepadogaster decandollei (GR, GAVG-138); Lepadogaster candollei (GD-119, GL-298, VJ). M. *Buwaħħal rasu twila*. Buwaħħal (GR, GAVG-138, GD-119, GL-298); Buwaħħal tar-rigi (VJ). E. Connemara suckerfish (/Connemara clingfish). 5-7cm. Variable; olive green or greenish brown with yellow and white spots; head streaked or spotted red, sometimes green and gold; fins reddish; males more red, females more green. Frequent. Pl.41(male).

286. **Lepadogaster lepadogaster** (Bonn.) Lepadogaster gouanii (GD-118, GL-297); Lepadogaster lepadogaster (JB, VJ). M. *Buwaħħal tat-tentakli*. Buwaħħal (GD-118, GL-297, JB); Buwaħħal tat-tikek (VJ). E. Suckerfish. 5-6cm. Grey or reddish grey with some ventral rows or scattered brownish or red spots. The species in our area belongs to the subspecies lepadogaster. Frequent. Pl.41.

Fam. Lophiidae

Body scaleless, all dorso-ventrally compressed, anteriorly very widened, tapering back towards an insignificant tail; pectorals spreading sideways; eyes on top of the wide, spiny head; mouth large, with numerous, thin teeth, lower jaw much longer than the upper; 1st dorsal modified into a decoy spine, anterior to and between eyes. Rays of 2nd dorsal 9 or 10, pectorals chisel-shaped: 287; rays of 2nd dorsal 11 0r 12, pectorals rounded and large: 288.

287. **Lophius budegassa** Spin. Lophius budegassa (GR, GAVG-154, GD-272, GL-301, JB). M. *Petriċa żgħira*. Petriċa (GR, GAVG-154, GD-272, GL-301); Petriċa tat-tbajja (JB). E. Lesser anglerfish 30-50cm.+. Reddish brown or brownish with small white spots. Formerly often used to be considered as the juvenile form of Lophius piscatorius Linn. Frequent. Pl.41.

288. **Lophius piscatorius** Linn. Lophius piscatorius (GT, GR, GAVG-153, GD-271, GL-300, JB). M. *Petriċa kbira*. Petriċa (GT, GR, GAVG-153, GD-271, GL-300, JB). E. Greater angler fish. 0.80-1.00m.+. Brownish or greenish brown, or ochrish brown; not uniform but mostly marbled. Frequent. Pl.41.

PLATE 1

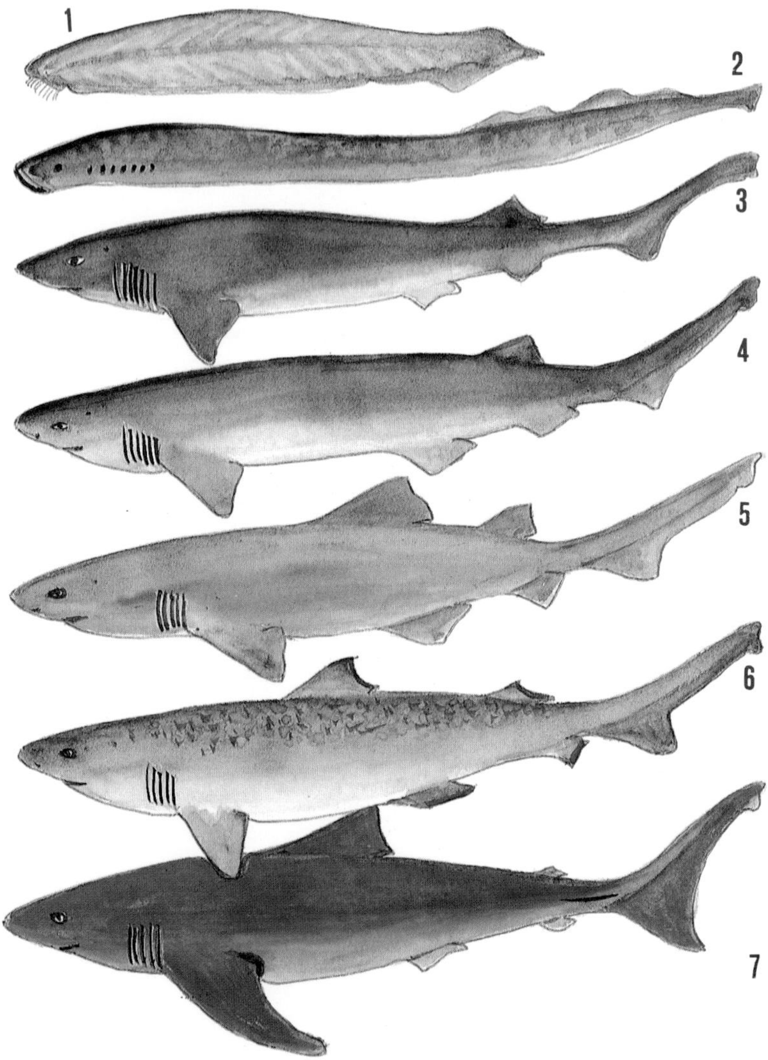

PLATE 2

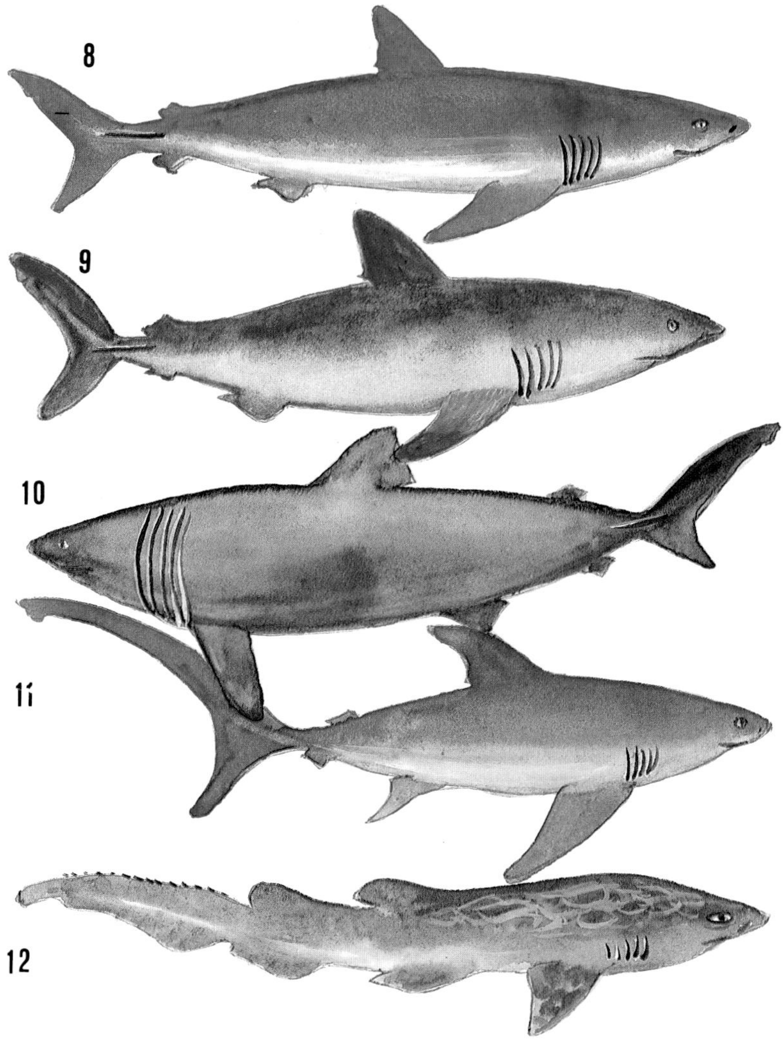

PLATE 3

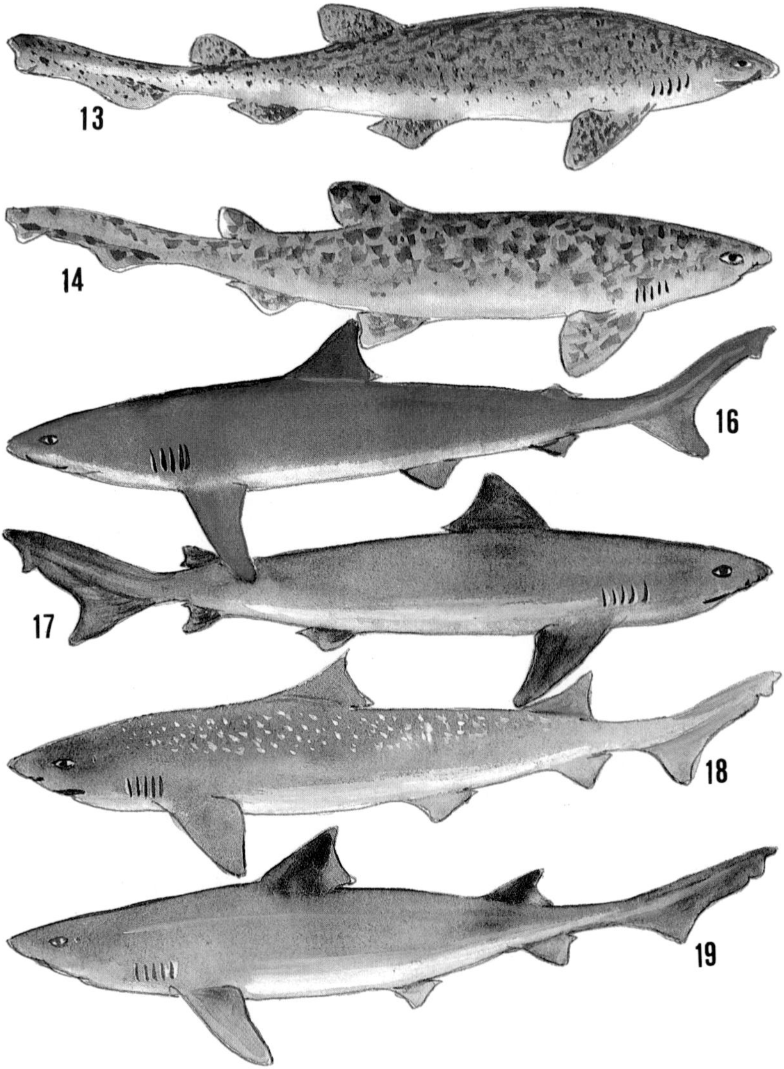

PLATE 4

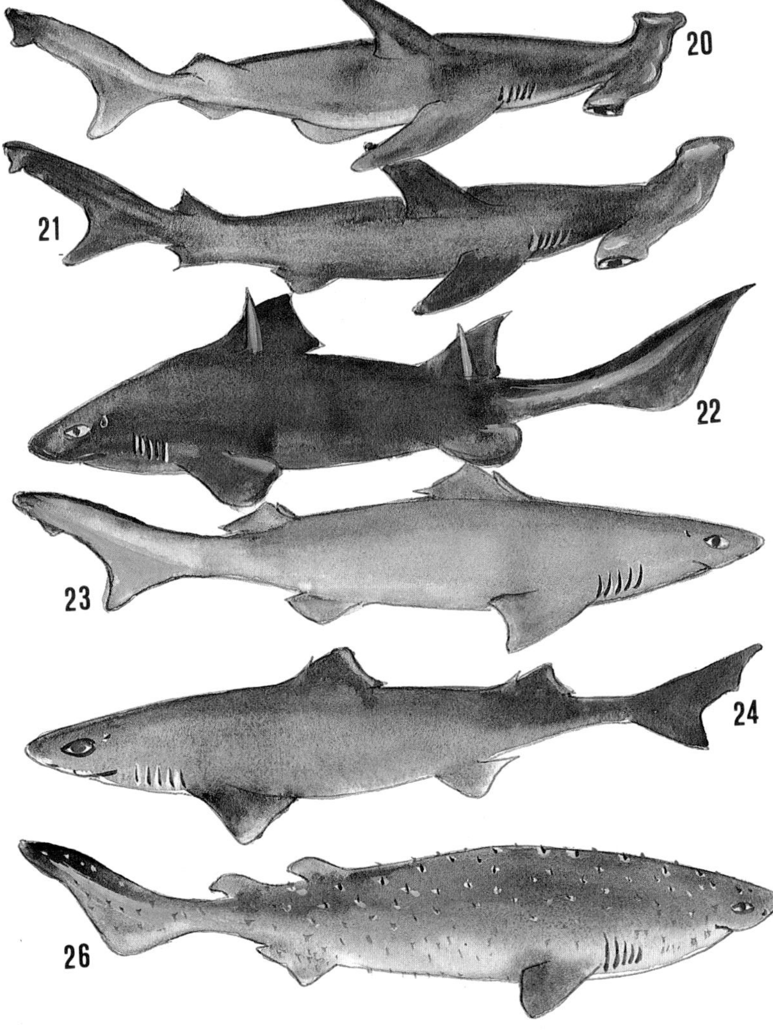

PLATE 5

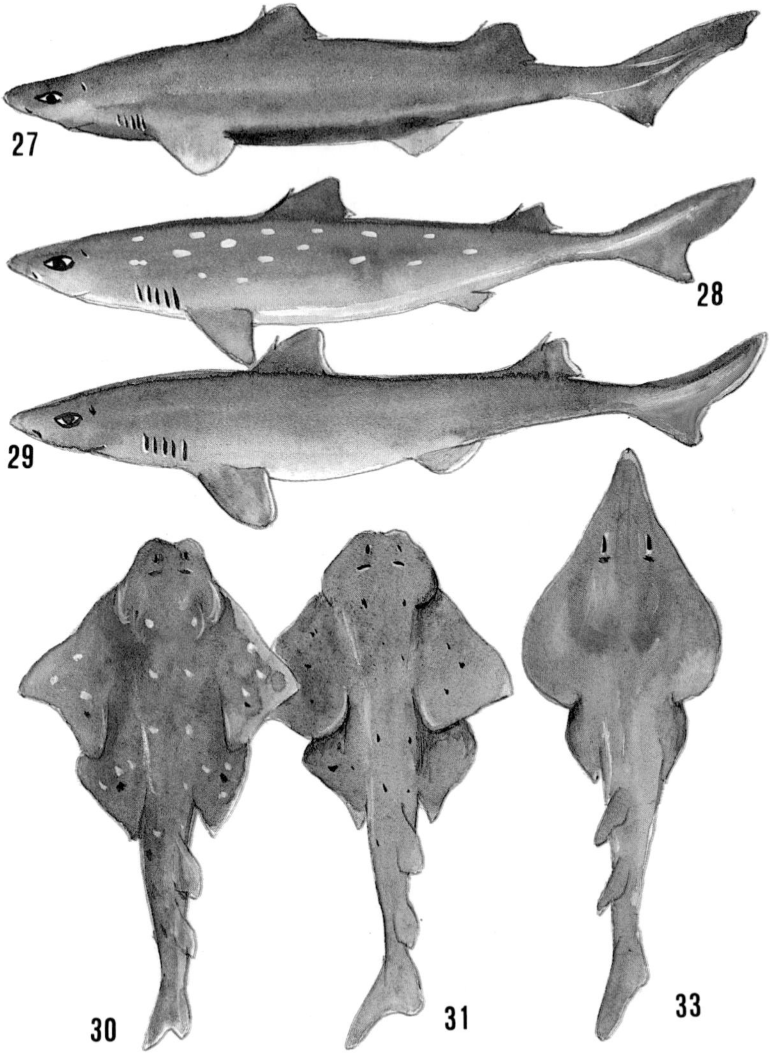

PLATE 6

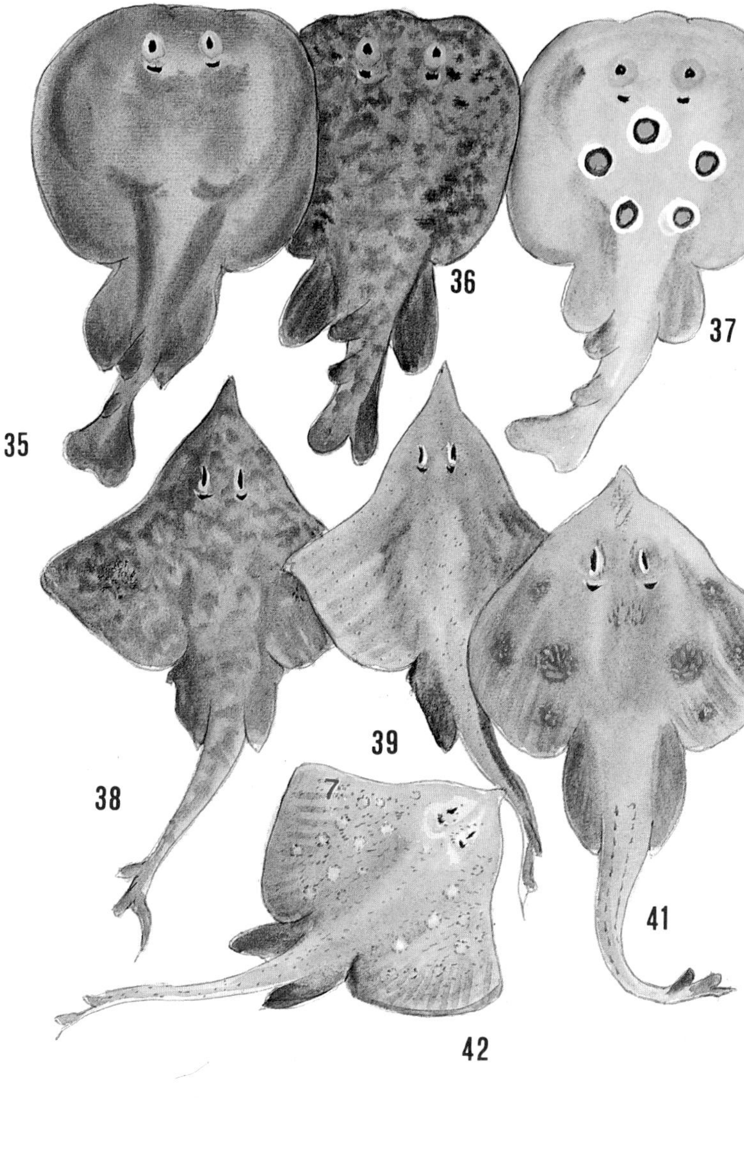

PLATE 7

PLATE 8

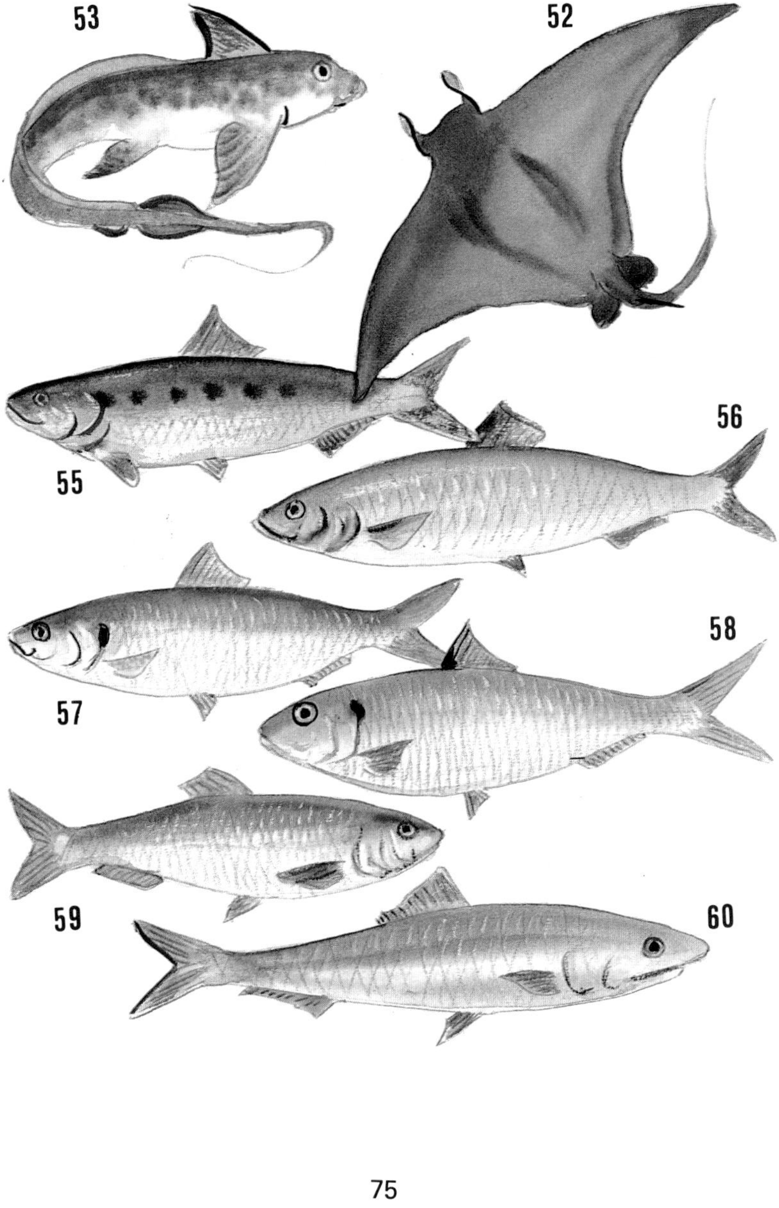

PLATE 9

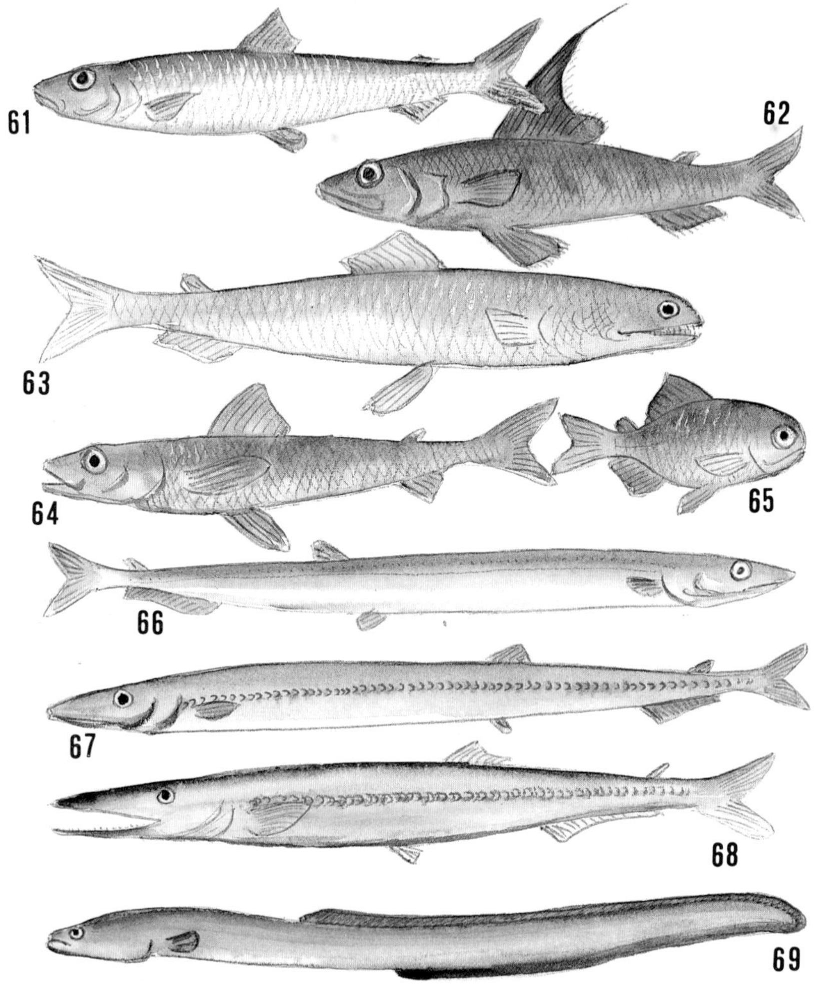

PLATE 10

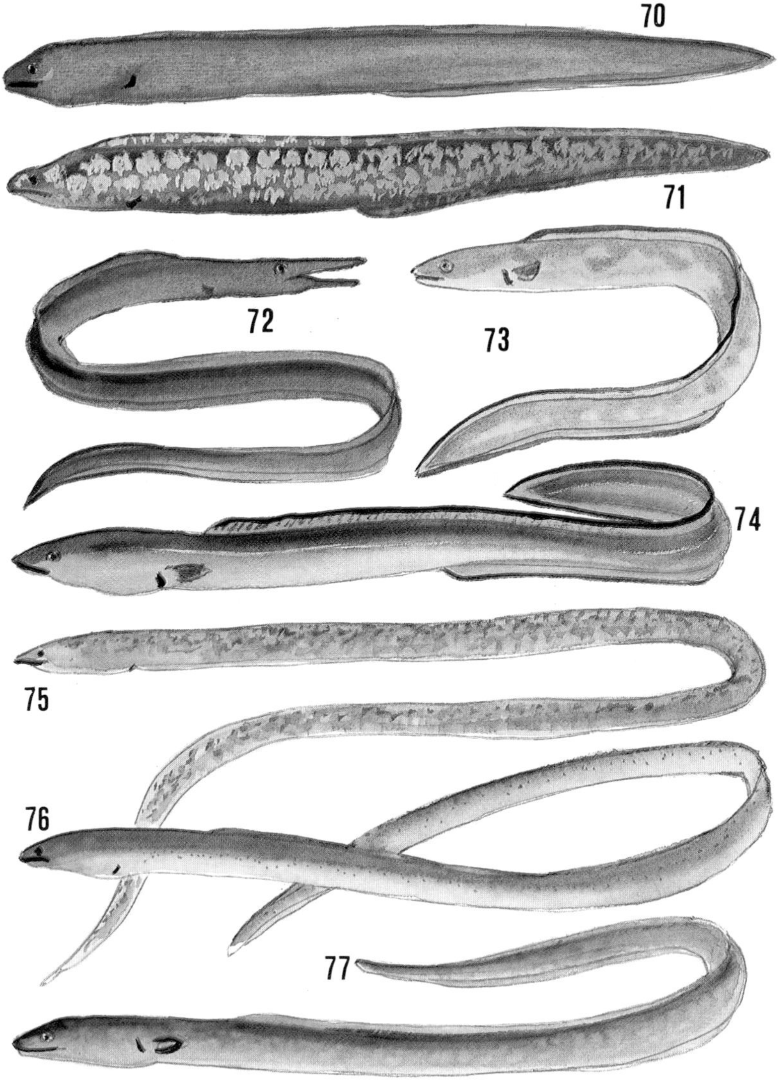

PLATE 11

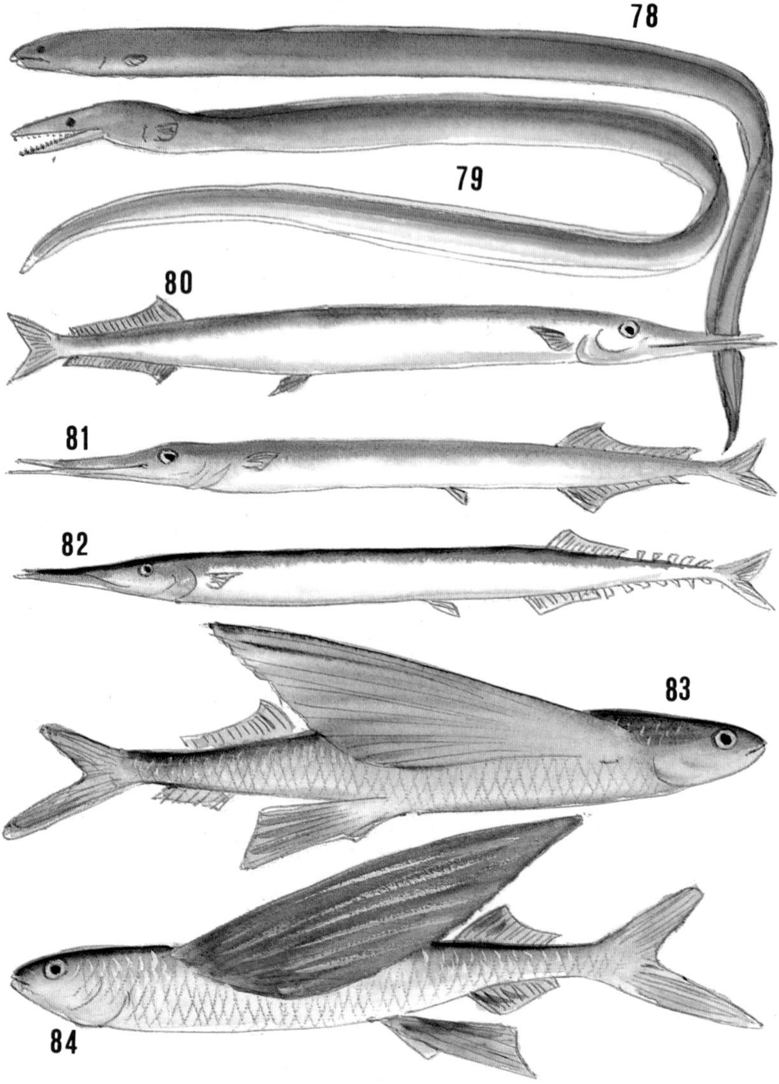

PLATE 12

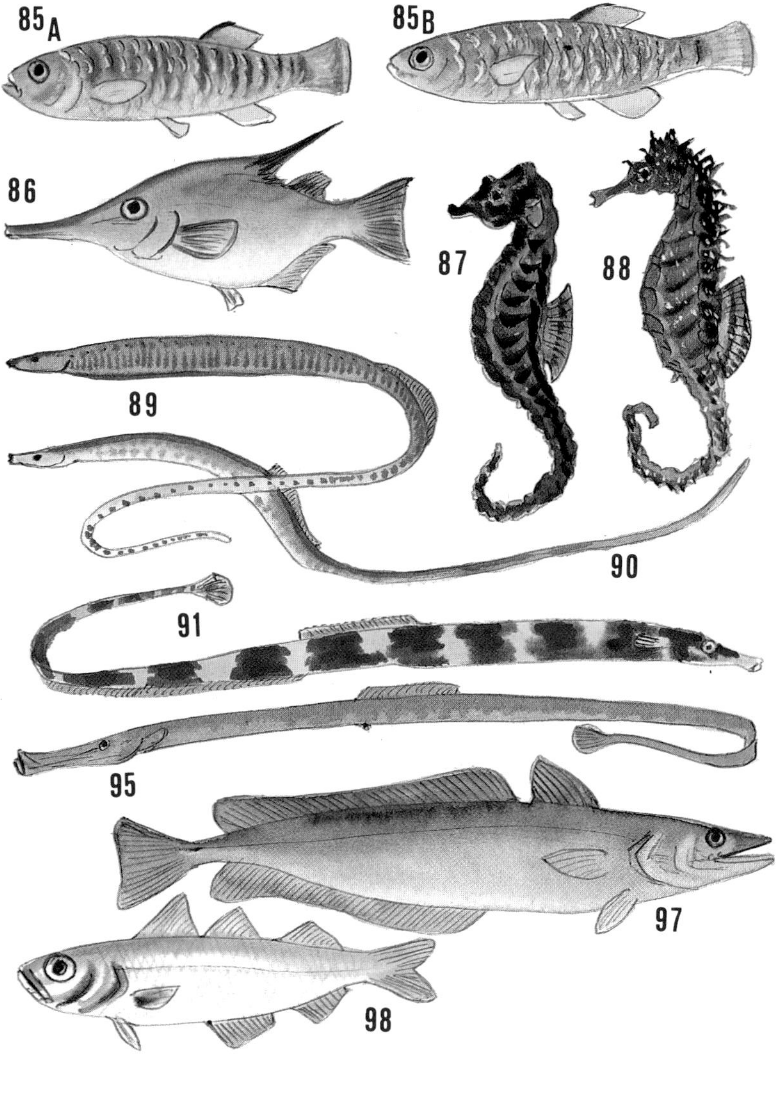

PLATE 13

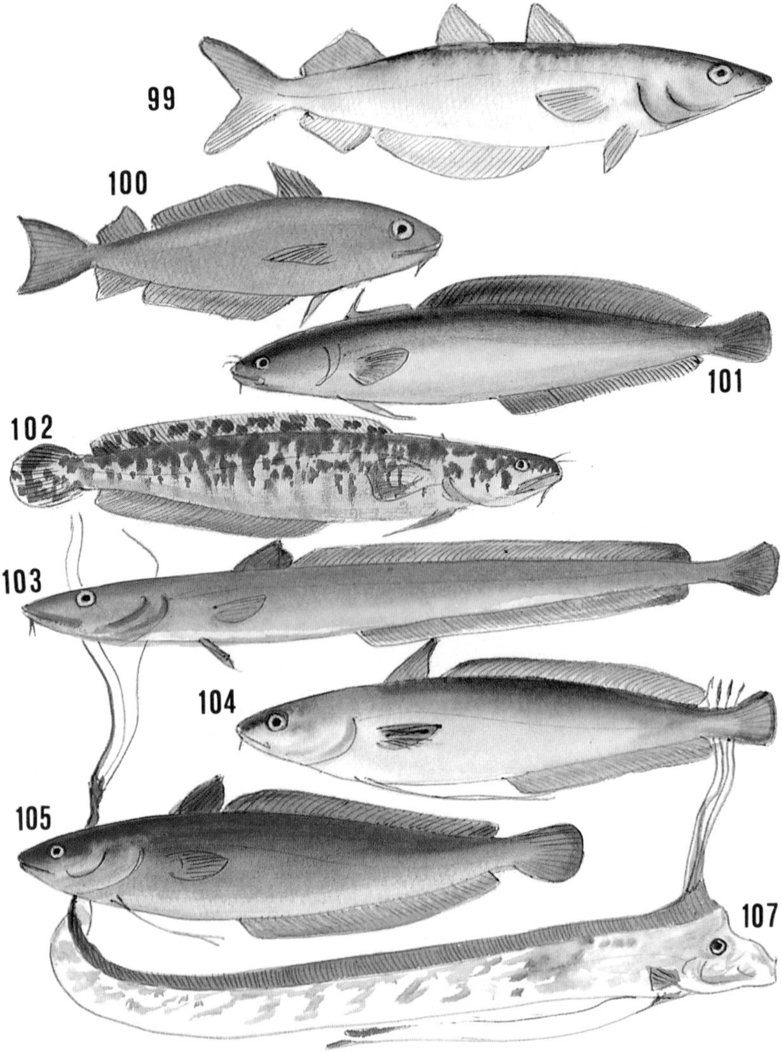

PLATE 14

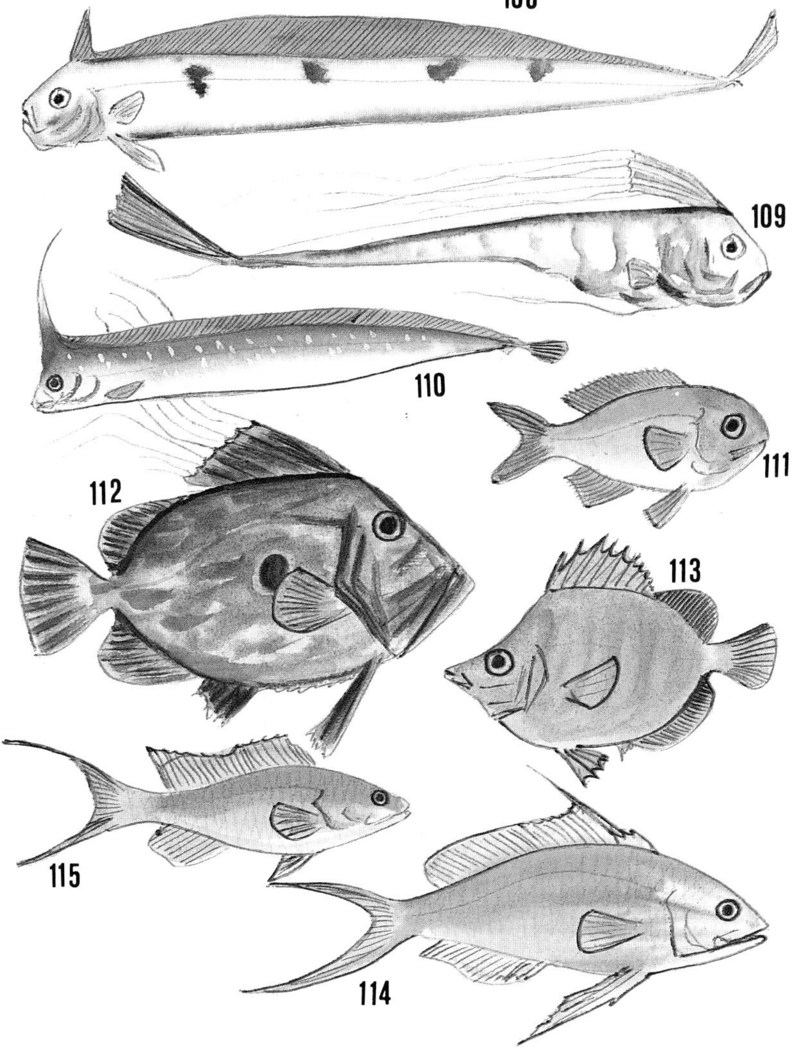

PLATE 15

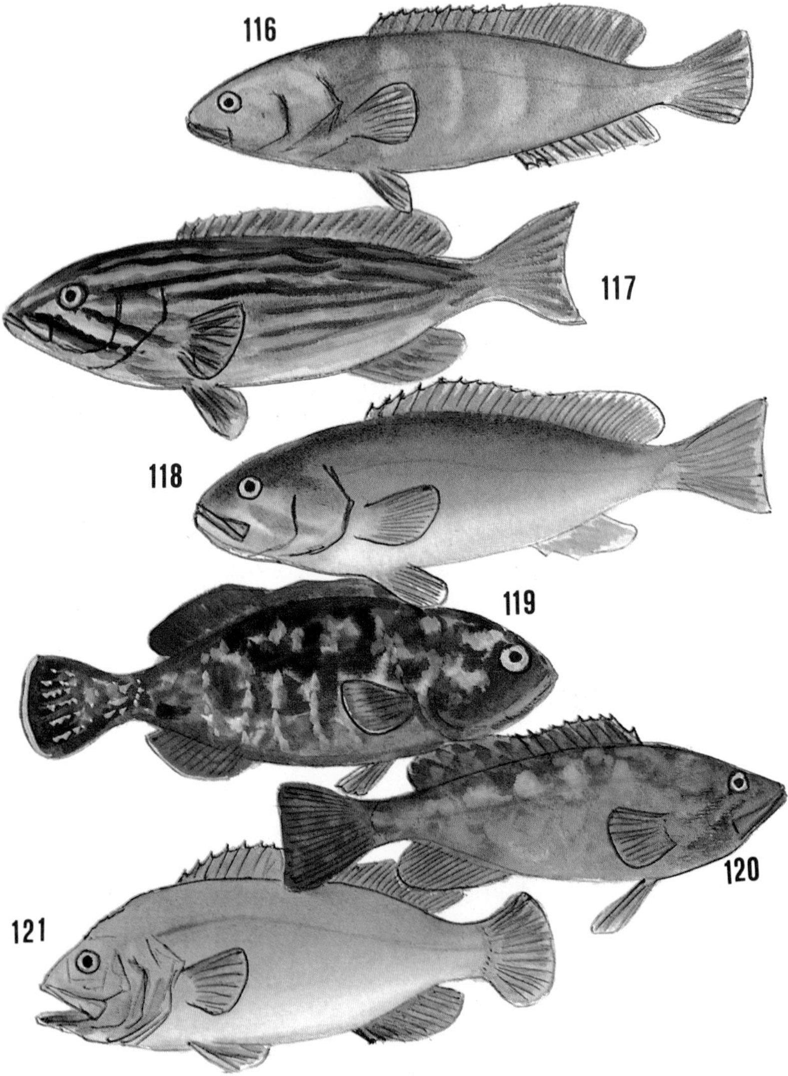

PLATE 16

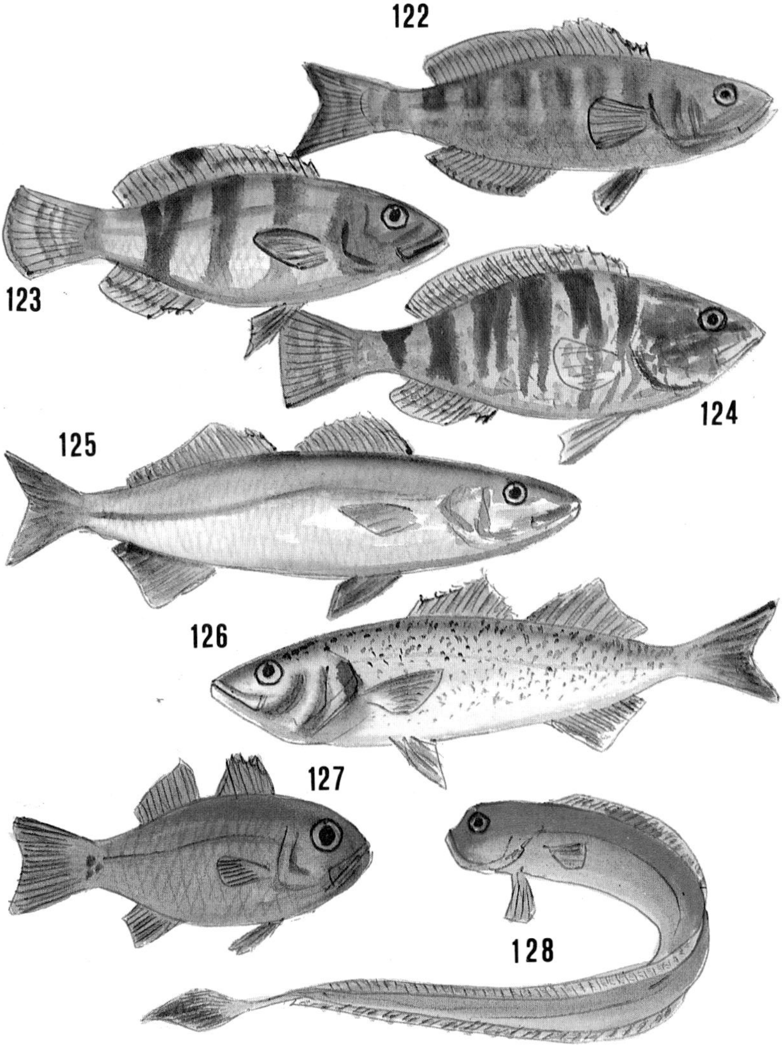

PLATE 17

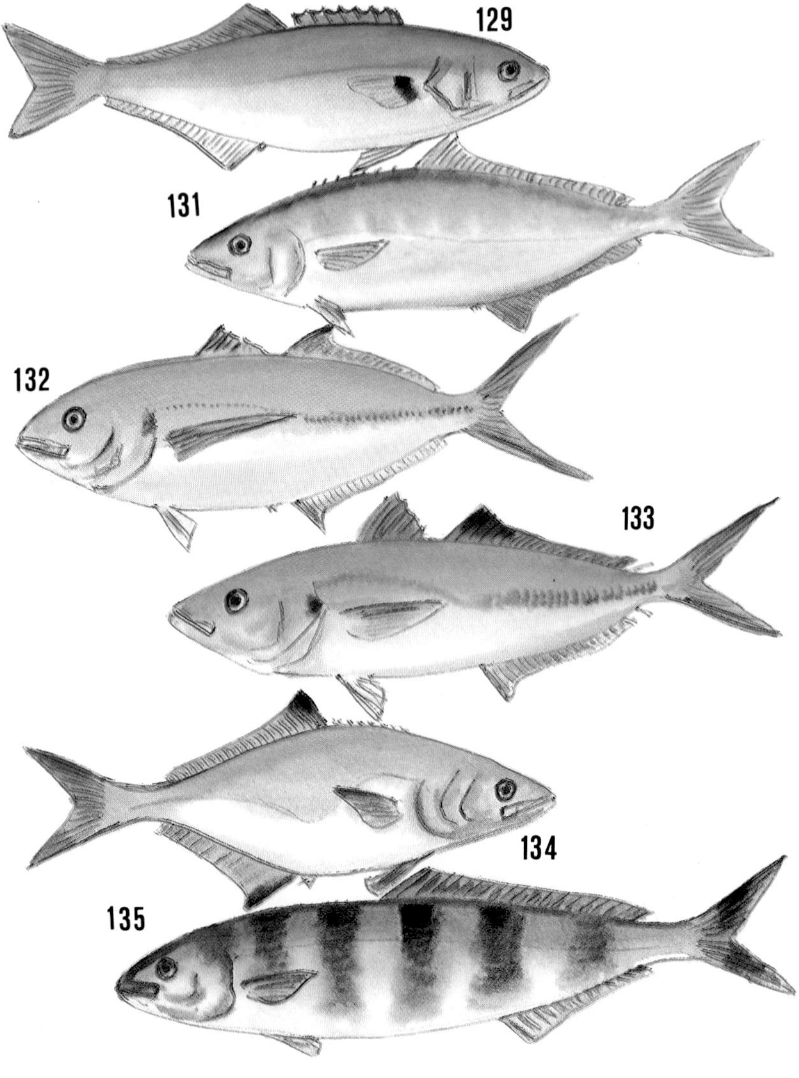

PLATE 18

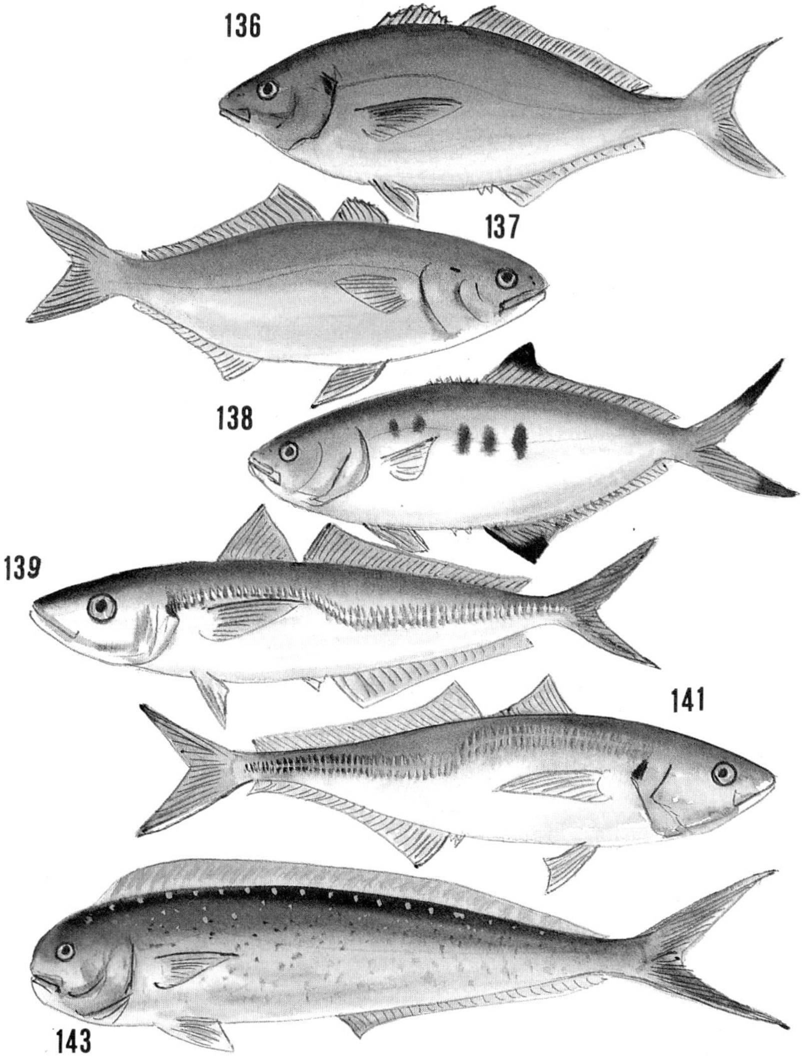

PLATE 19

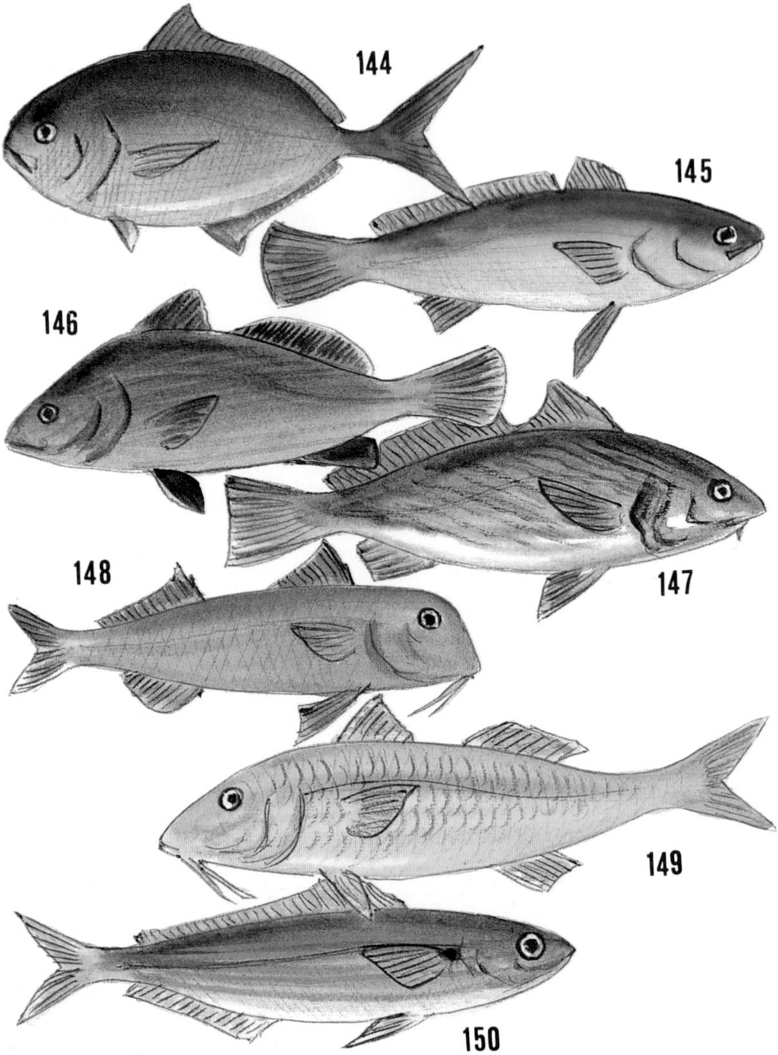

PLATE 20

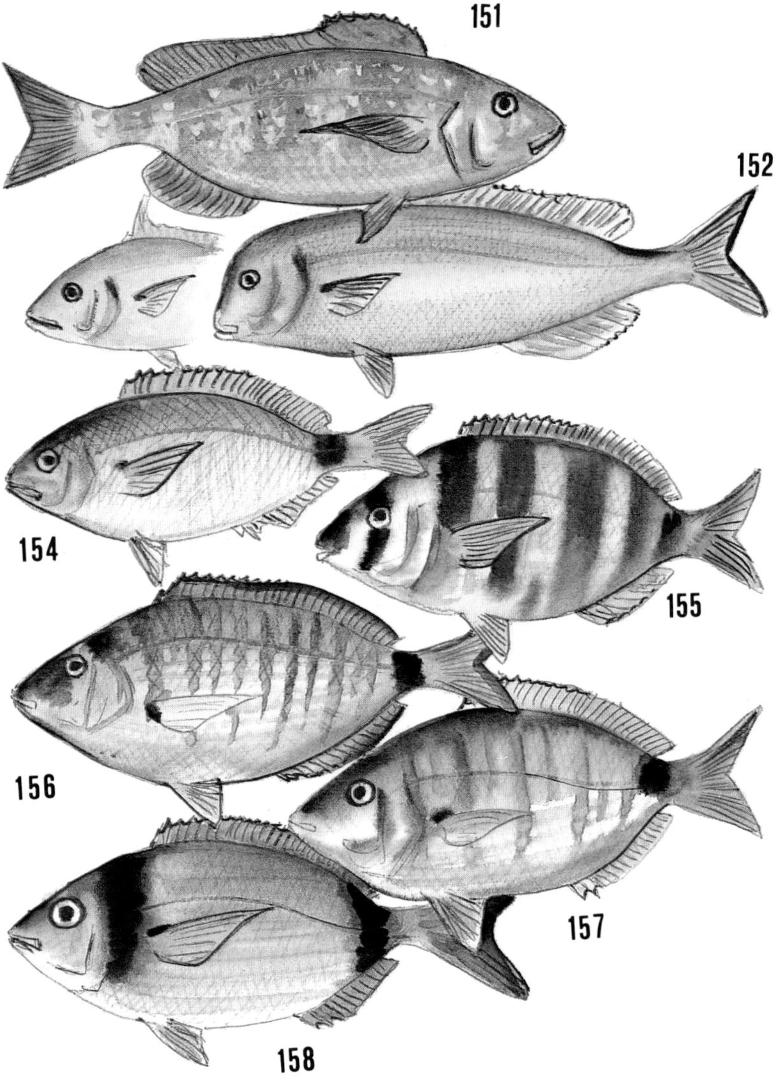

PLATE 21

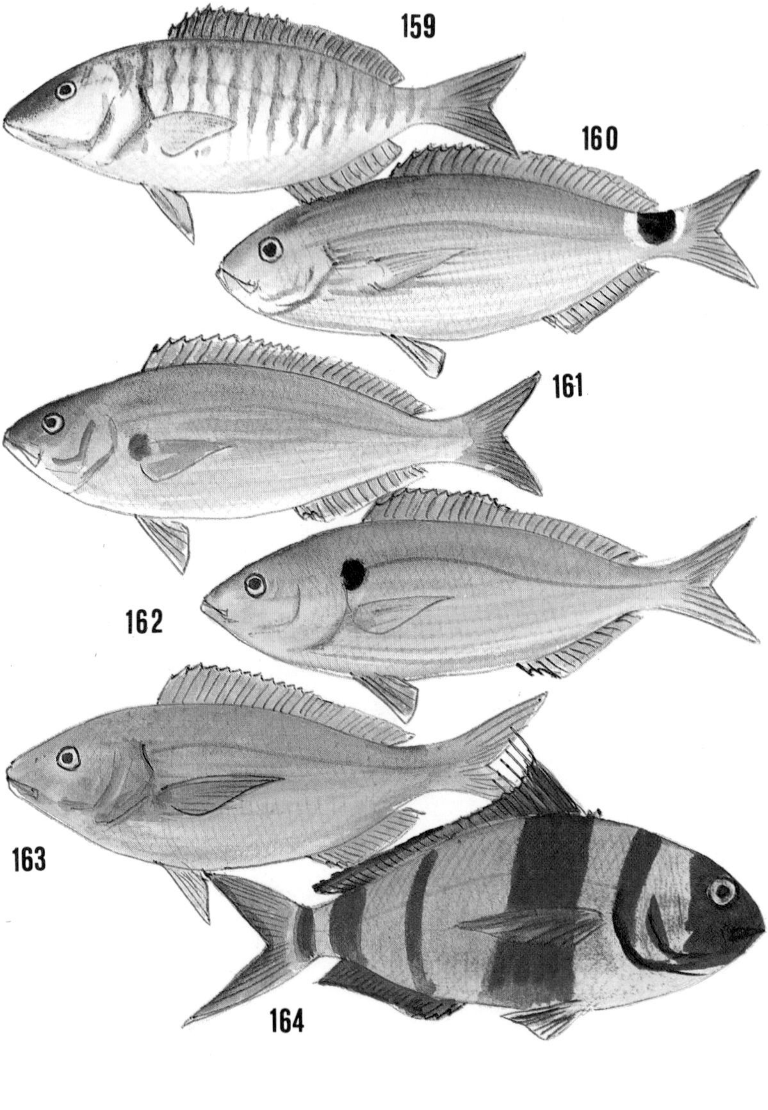

PLATE 22

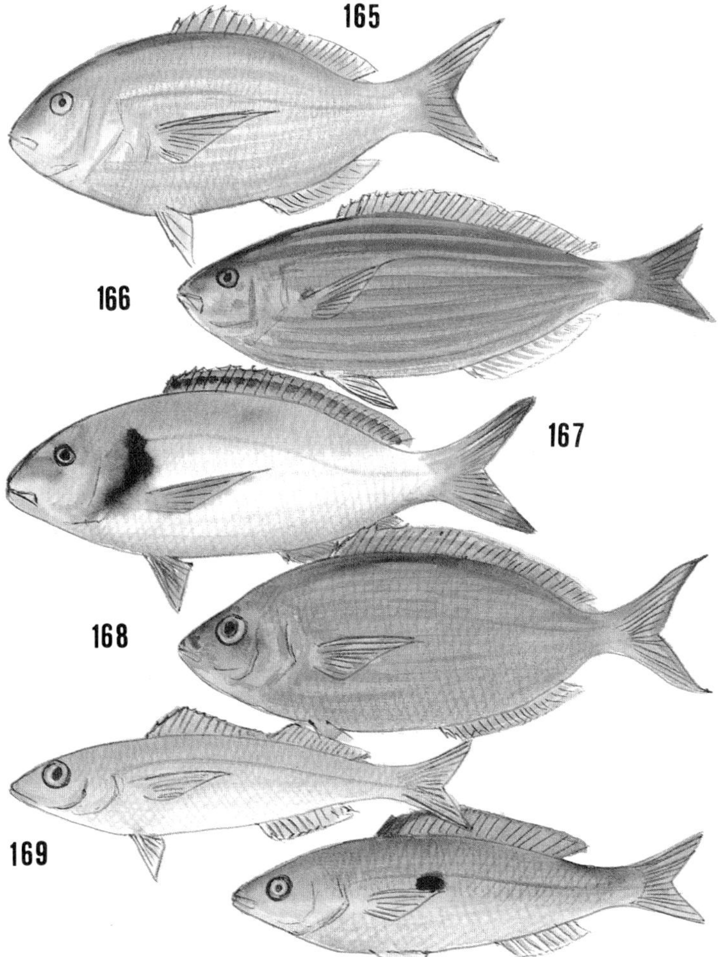

PLATE 23

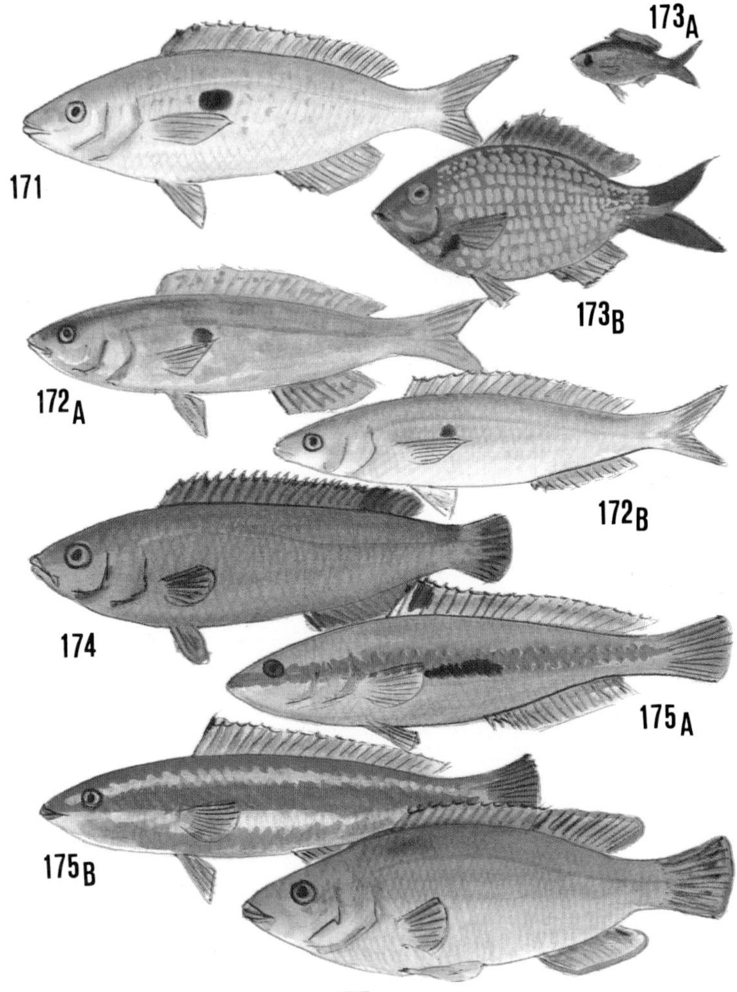

PLATE 24

176A
178
176B
179
180
181

PLATE 25

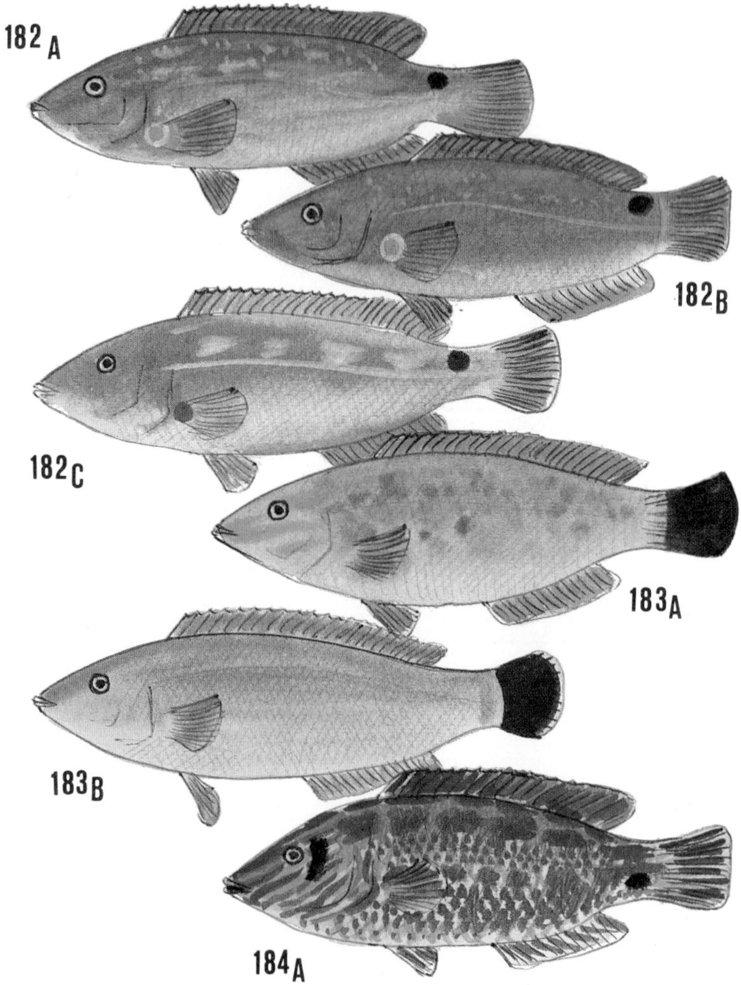

PLATE 26

PLATE 27

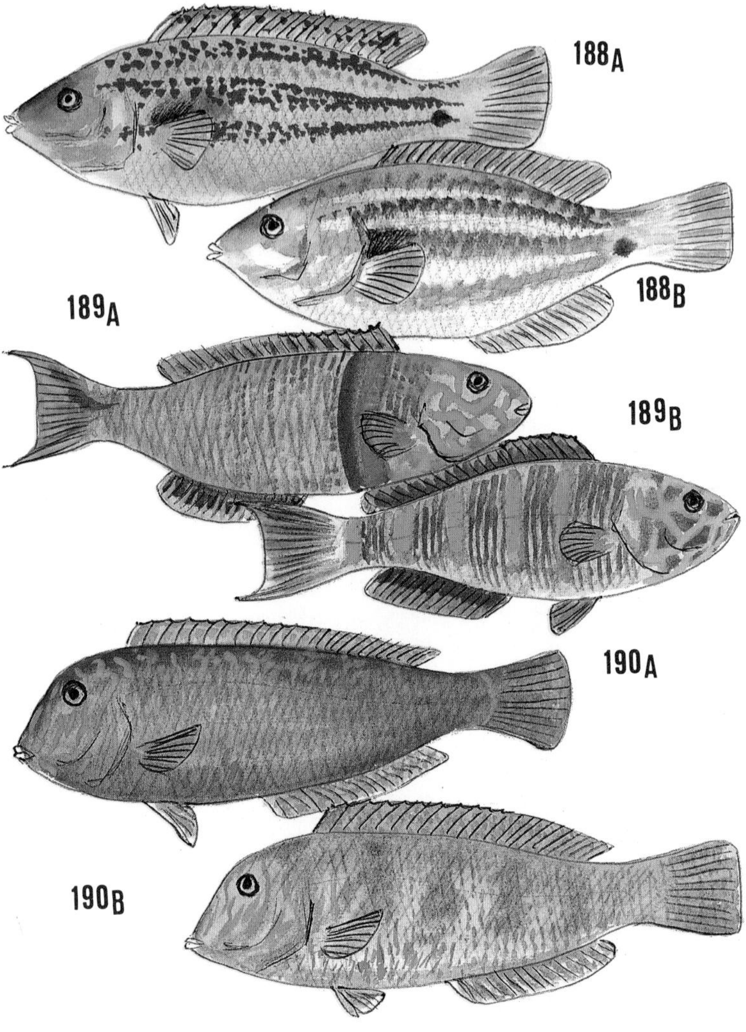

PLATE 28

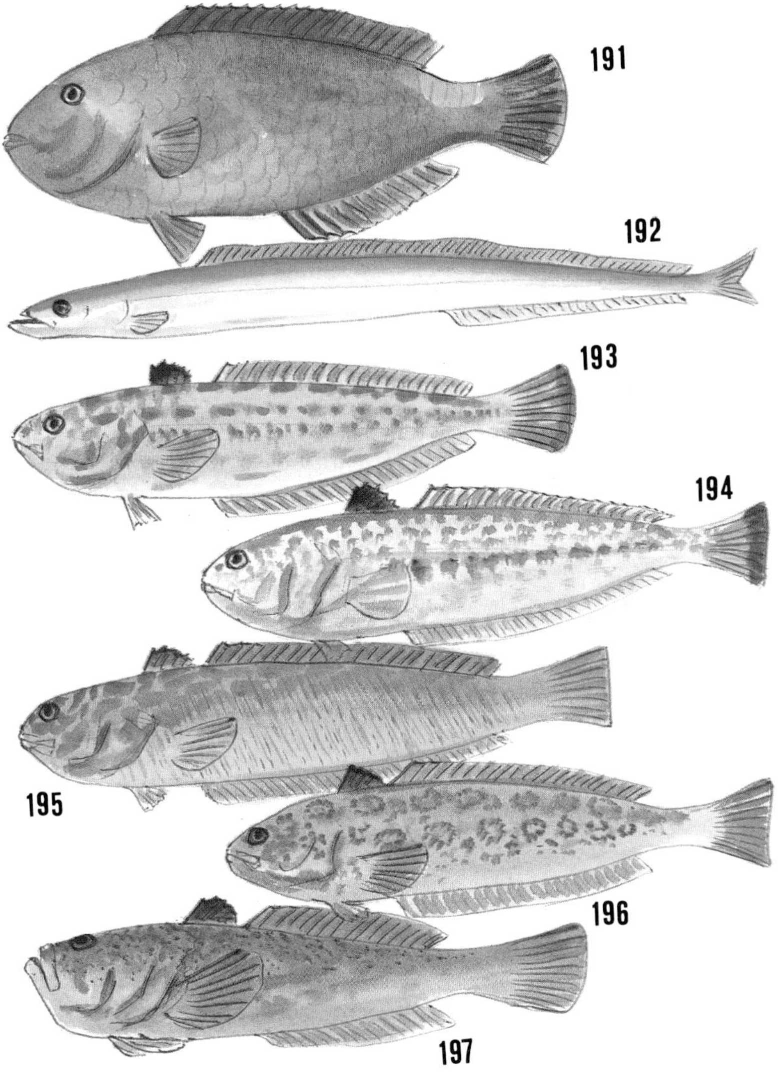

PLATE 29

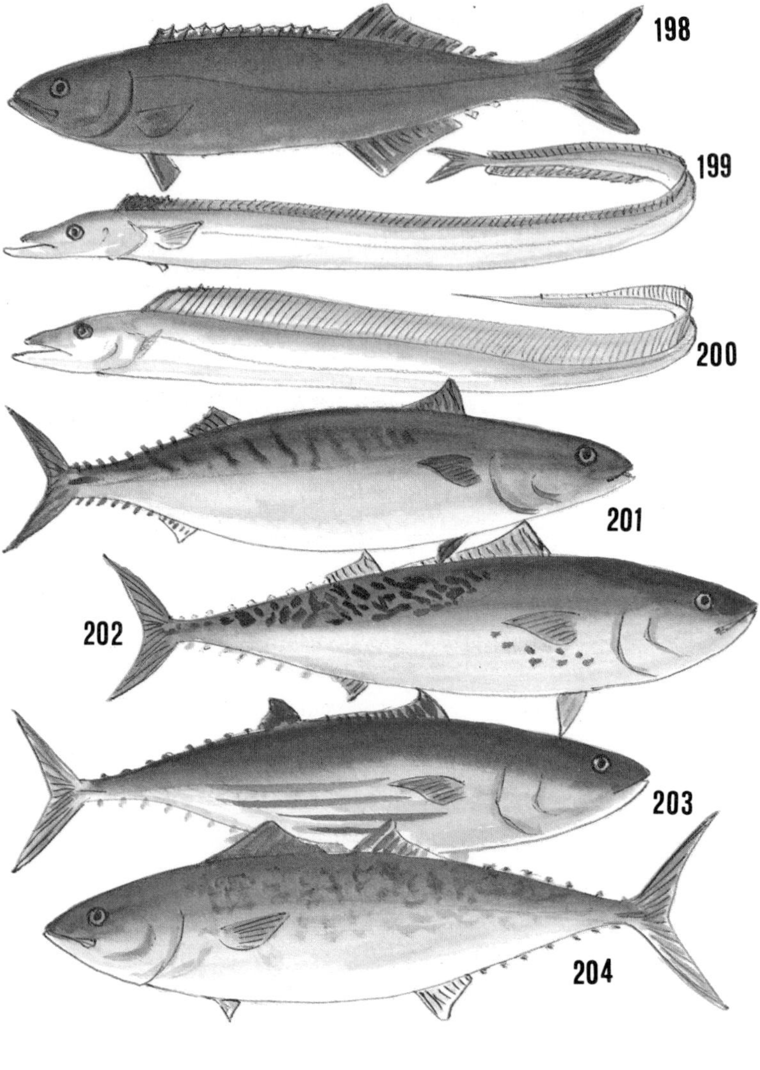

PLATE 30

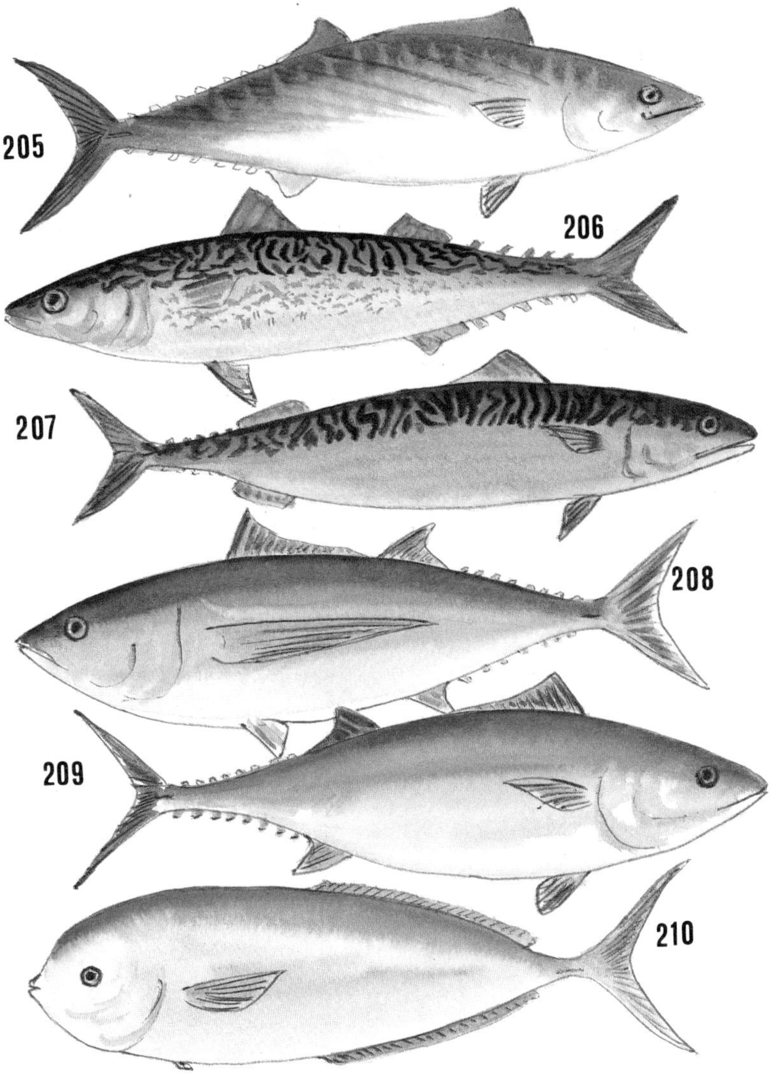

PLATE 31

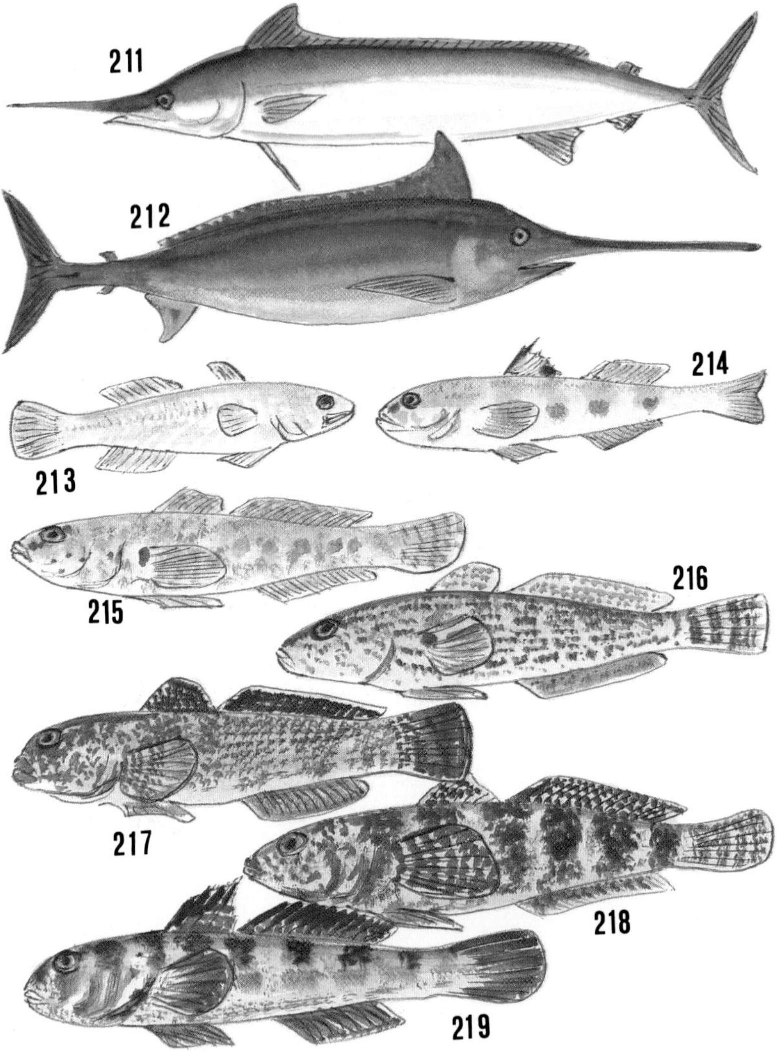

PLATE 32

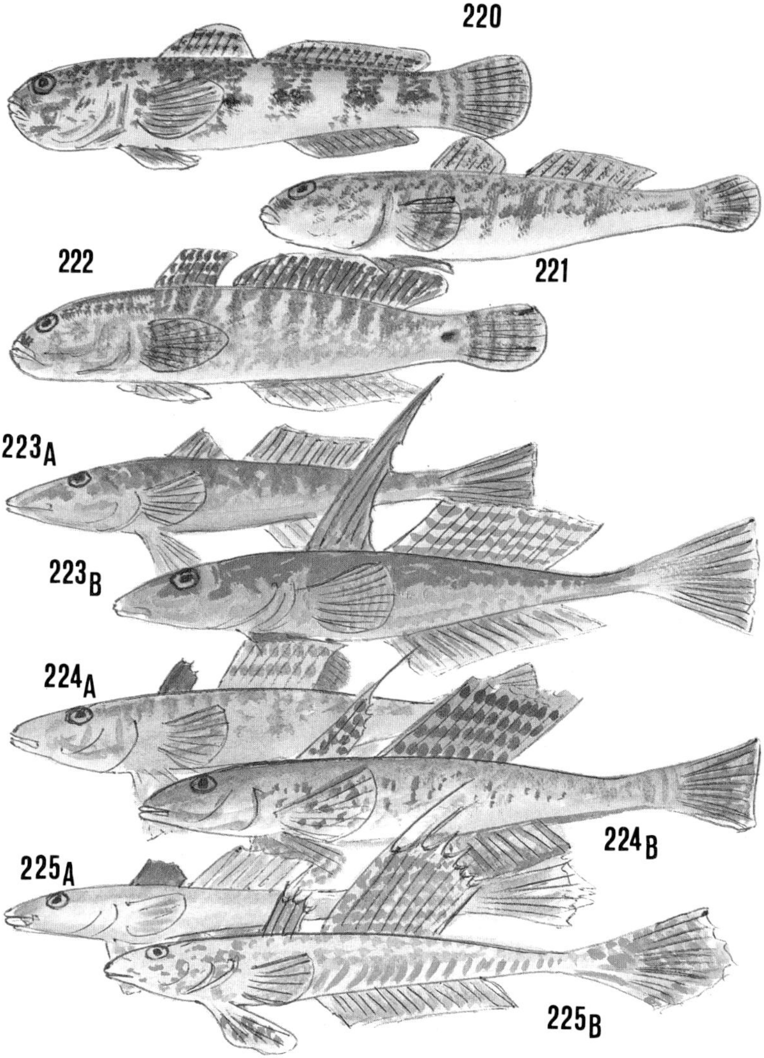

PLATE 33

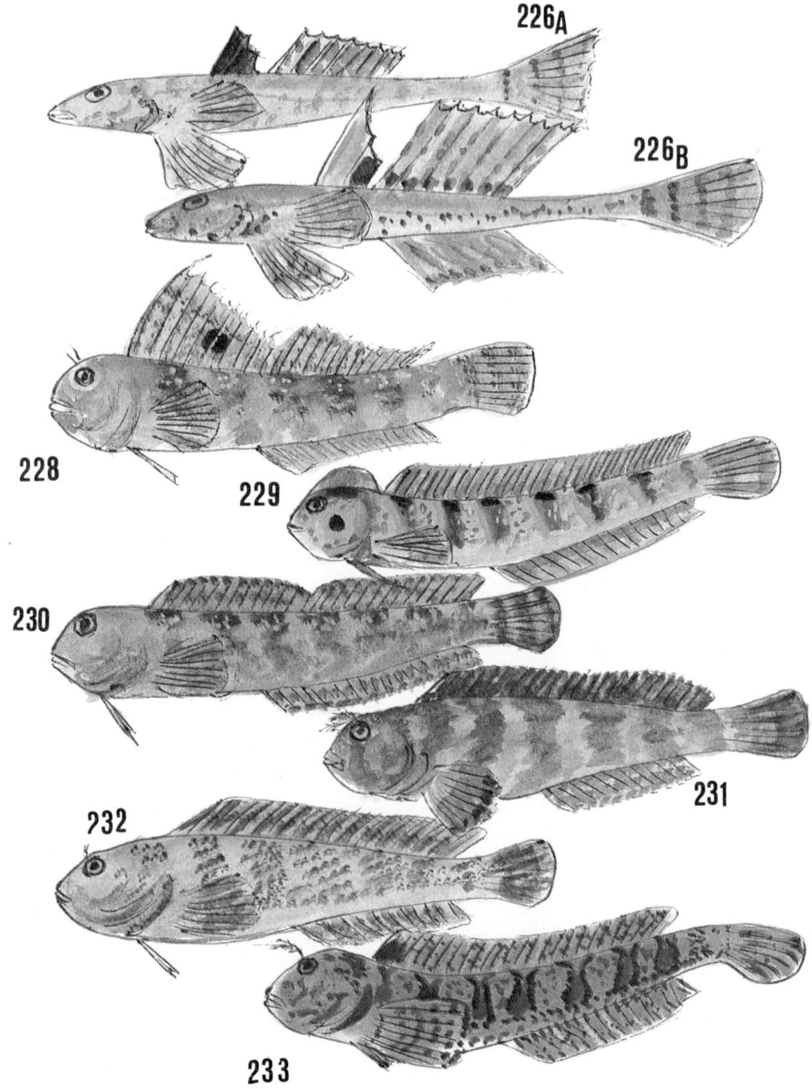

PLATE 34

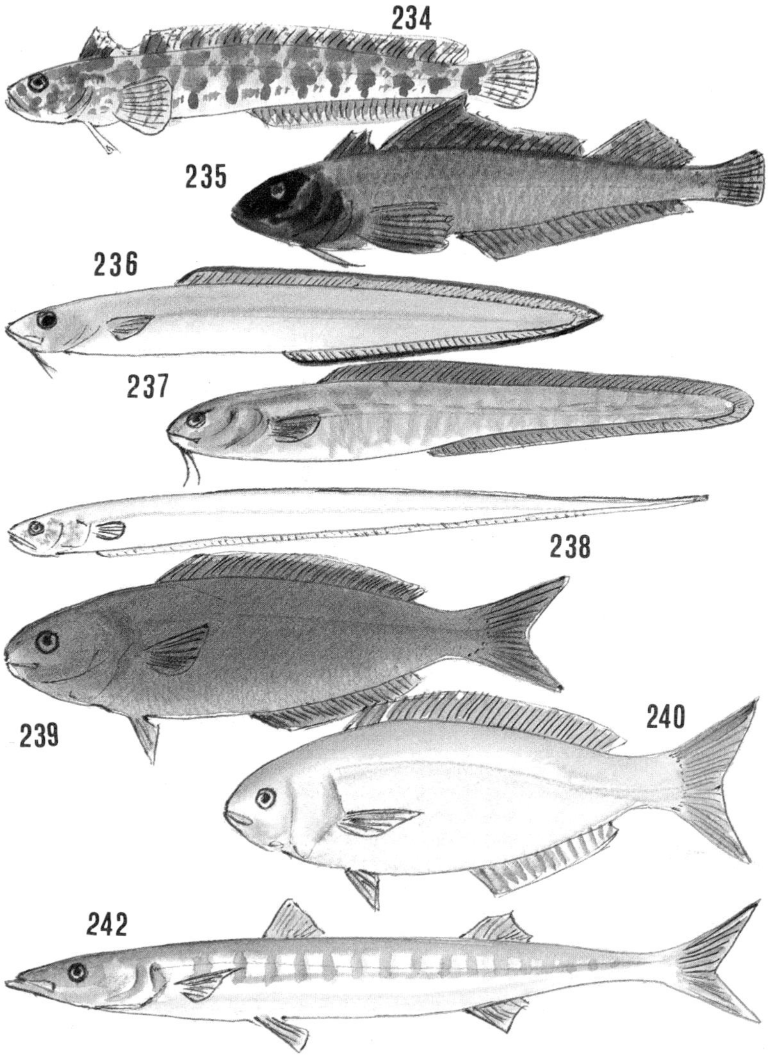

PLATE 35

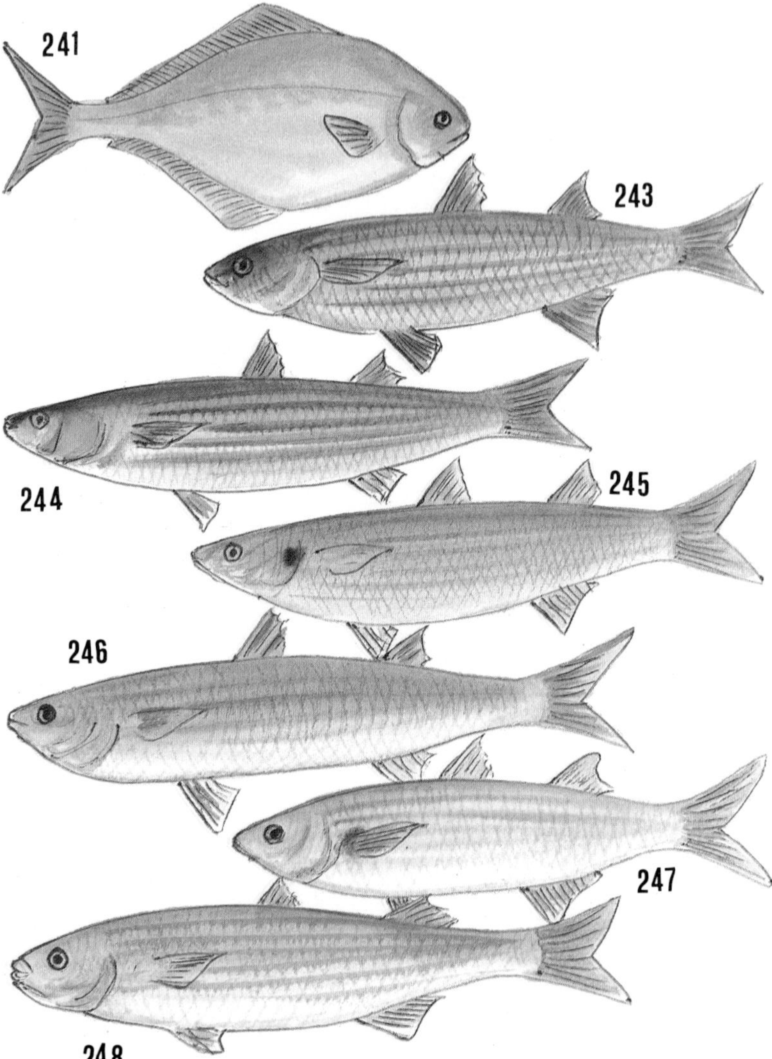

PLATE 36

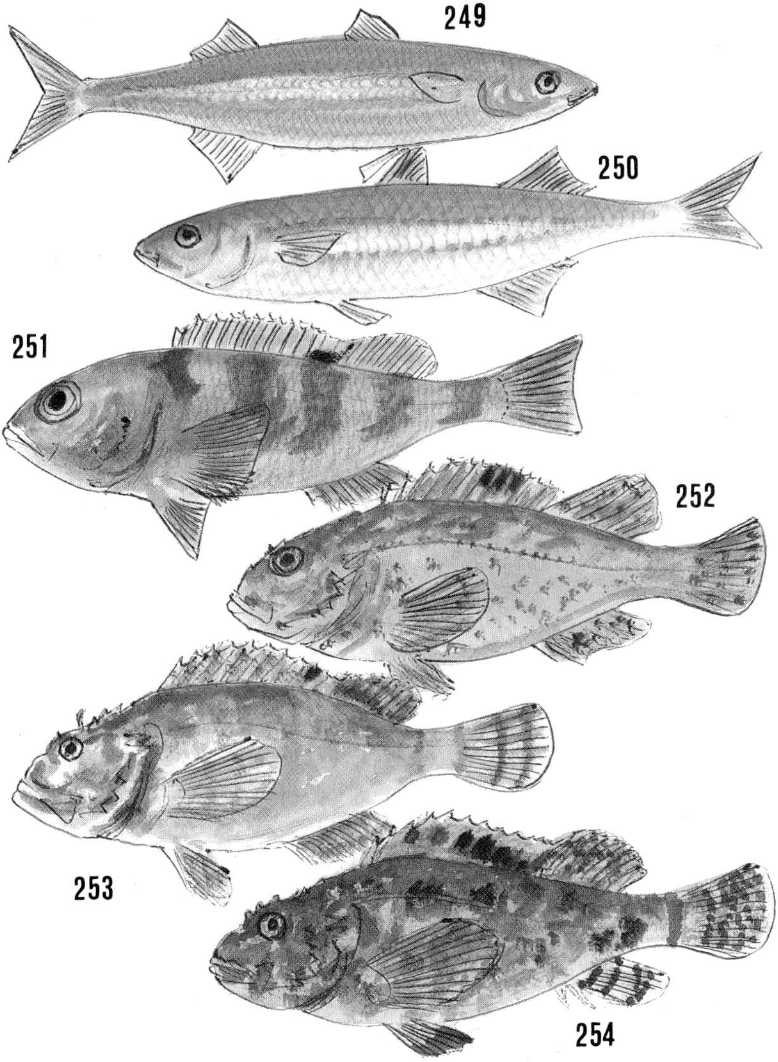

PLATE 37

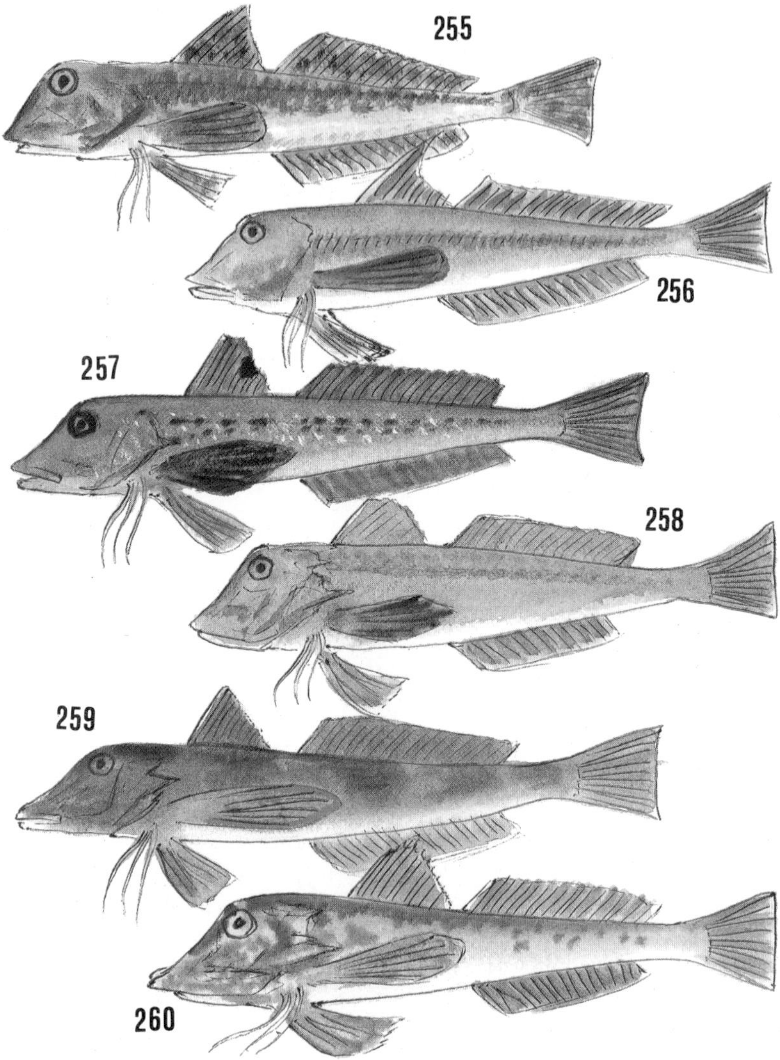

PLATE 38

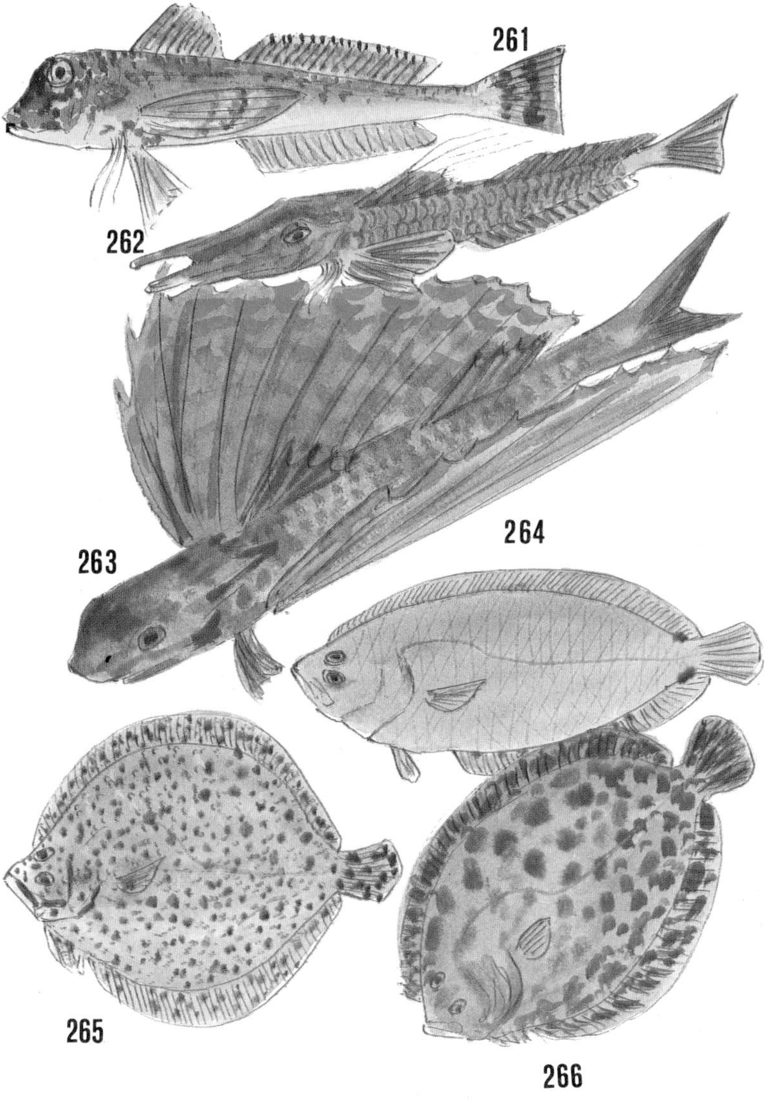

PLATE 39

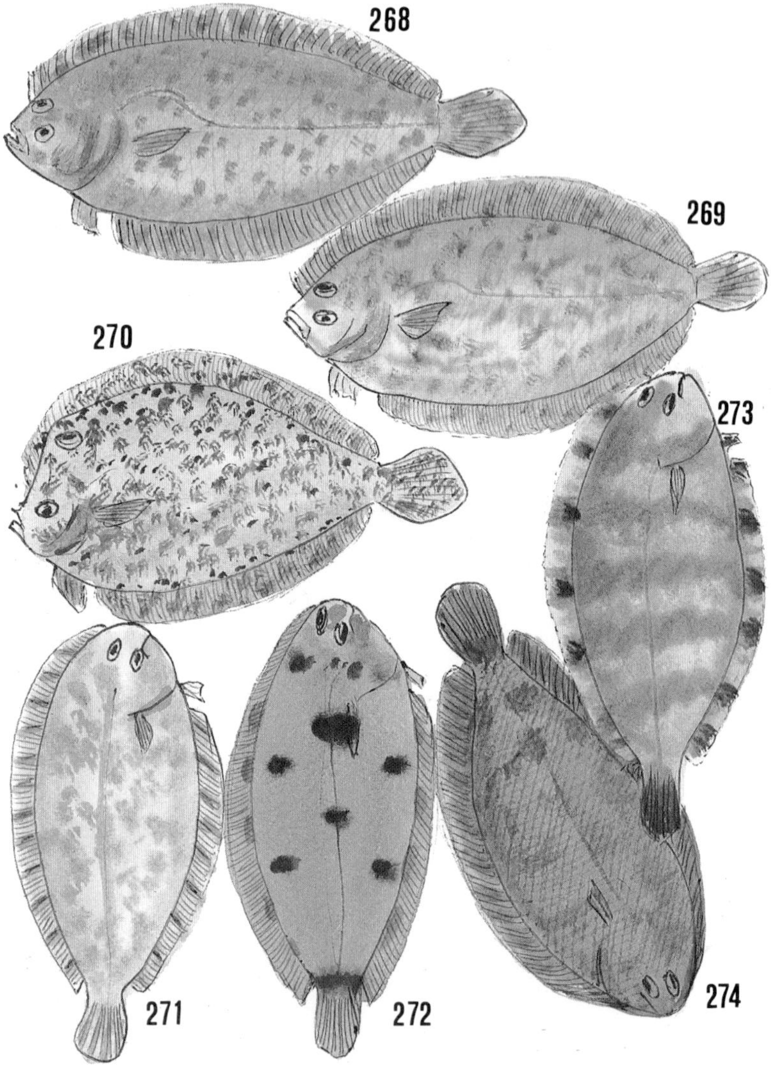

PLATE 40

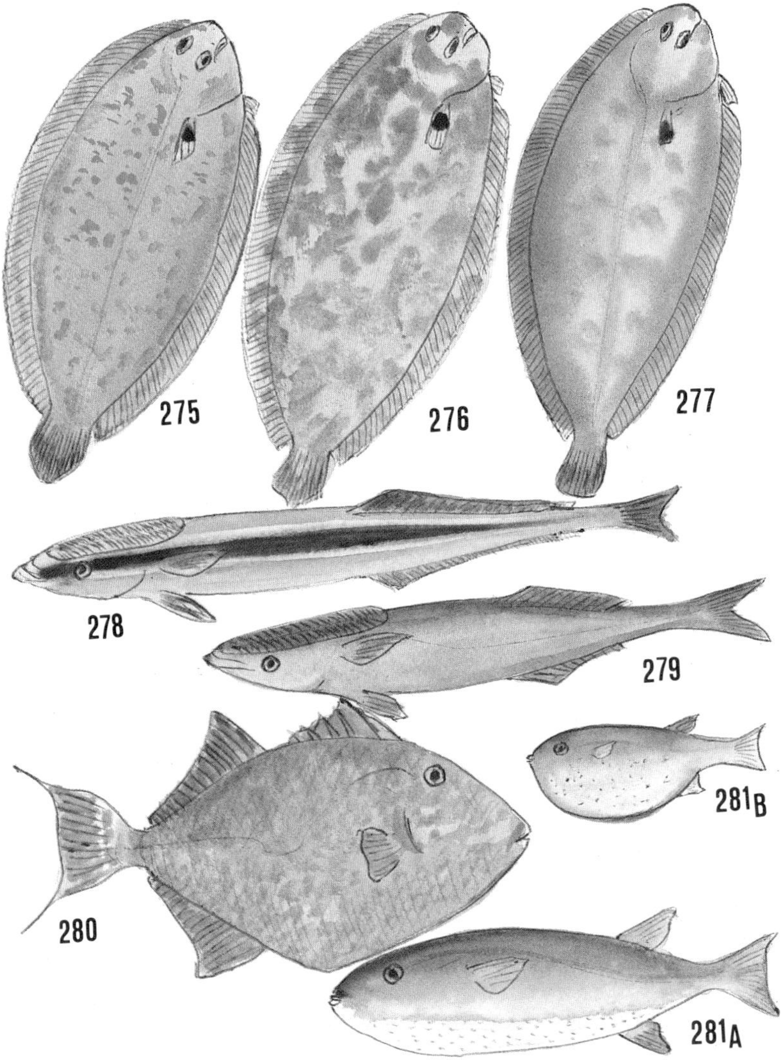

PLATE 41

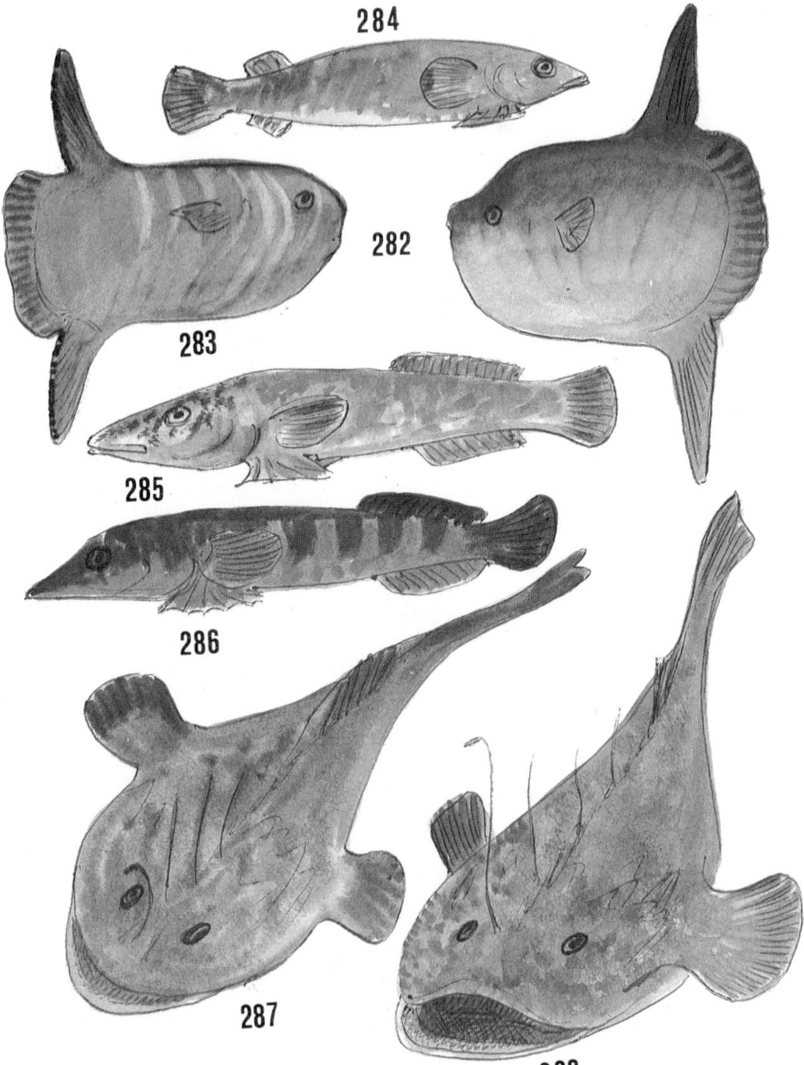

INDEX

Numbers refer to paragraphs in the text, and not to pages. Block letters denote fish families, bold type are the principal scientific names, italics represent principal Maltese names. Normal type is for English names, synonymous or secondary technical and Maltese names.